Life Spirit

For groups and individuals
exploring deep questions

David Usher

Published by The Lindsey Press, London,
on behalf of The Hibbert Trust

a unitarian publication

Published by the Lindsey Press
(The General Assembly of Unitarian and Free Christian Churches
Essex Hall, 1–6 Essex Street, London WC2R 3HY, UK)

on behalf of The Hibbert Trust

© The Hibbert Trust 2015

ISBN 978-0-85319-085-1

Designed and typeset by Garth Stewart

Printed and bound in the United Kingdom by
Lightning Source, Milton Keynes

Contents

Note to the reader

Life Spirit is sponsored by **The Hibbert Trust**, which was established in the mid-nineteenth century for the promotion of free and open religious enquiry. In providing this course, the Trust does not aim to convert anyone to a particular way of thinking, or to persuade anyone to join a particular faith. The Trust is committed to the idea that spirituality is about having an intelligent personal faith, honestly considered and thoughtfully lived – which is important for the world, as well as for the quality of the individual life.

David Usher, the author, has a Master's Degree in Philosophy and Theology from the University of Oxford, and a Doctorate in Ministry from Andover Newton Theological School in Boston, Massachusetts. He has been a Unitarian minister since 1981, serving congregations in the United Kingdom until 1990 and then in the United States until 2000, when he returned to the UK. After serving for seven years as District Minister for Unitarians in London and the South East, he resumed his congregational ministry in the United States in 2014. He is the author of *Twelve Steps to Spiritual Health* (The Lindsey Press, 2013).

The Lindsey Press, the publisher, is associated with the General Assembly of Unitarian and Free Christian Churches. Unitarianism is a progressive faith whose historical roots are in Christianity but which embraces truths from all religious and philosophical traditions. It emphasises the primacy of individual reason, conscience, and experience in matters of faith, and it is strongly committed to social action and human rights.

The Hibbert Trust
Registered Charity: 233121
www.thehibberttrust.org.uk

The General Assembly of Unitarian and Free Christian Churches
Registered Charity: 250788
www.unitarian.org.uk

Introduction

Life Spirit is designed to help you to explore some of the big questions about life, and to find some of your own answers. This could be done alone, as an individual, or (ideally) in the company of others who are seeking their own answers.

There are several reasons why you might be interested in this course. Perhaps you find yourself asking questions about your life, and how you can live it more meaningfully, with more attention to your spiritual health and well-being; but you don't like being told what to believe, and many of the things that traditional churches tell you to believe seem to you to be unbelievable. You want to nurture your spirit, but you don't want to compromise your intelligence. You want to be free to believe what you think is true, and not believe what you think is not true. And you want to be free to choose which spiritual practices suit you.

If that describes you, *Life Spirit* is for you. In *Life Spirit* you will be expected to think for yourself.

Have you ever asked questions like these:

- *Does my life have meaning?*
- *Why am I here?*
- *What will happen when I die?*
- *How can I find a compass to guide me through life's difficult moral choices?*
- *How can I find spiritual strength and faith?*
- *Why is there suffering?*
- *Is there a God?*

If you have ever wondered about any of these questions, you are in good company. People have been asking those questions since the dawn of human consciousness.

Life Spirit is designed to help you explore these questions and more. But it will not tell you the answers. It is not spiritual fast food which might give you a quick rush of enjoyment but does not give you lasting nourishment. *Life Spirit* is designed to nourish your soul. It will help you to explore not only what you believe, but also why you believe it, and what those beliefs mean to you, and ideally to do so in community with others who are seeking to formulate their own beliefs.

Life Spirit is not just about thinking and beliefs. It is also about feeling and experiencing – and going beyond feeling and experiencing, allowing yourself to enter a space beyond the head and even the heart, simply being in a state of ultimate acceptance and trust in the universe. *Life Spirit* is also about what you *do* as a result of what you believe and feel and experience. It is about how you live so that your own life is spiritually enriched, and how to live so that the lives of others benefit from your spiritual enrichment.

Life Spirit is intended for anyone. Those following the course might have a background in organised religion, might have had some formal theological education, or might already have an active spiritual practice. Or they might be exploring these questions of ultimate importance for the first time. Some may bring knowledge and experience. Others will bring the freshness of an enquiring mind and heart.

The *Life Spirit* course is best done in a small group, because learning will come not only from each member's own reflections, but through interaction with the others in the group. In the spiritual quest, each one is both student and teacher. Each of us needs to have our spiritual ideas tested through dialogue and encounter with others. Those taking part learn from each other.

How does Life Spirit work?

There are twelve units. How long each will take will depend on how long your group wants to discuss the issues raised. It is strongly recommended that you start by doing Unit 1, called *Your Odyssey*, in which you are invited to tell the story of your own spiritual journey. It is important to understand how you got to where you are now before you embark upon the next phase of your journey. Then you may do any or all of the next ten units in whichever order you choose. Those ten units are as follows:

2. *What is Spirituality?* – Finding a way to express the inexpressible.
3. *The Role of Personal Faith.* – How does my personal faith influence my life?
4. *The Role of Organised Religion* – Do I really have to go to church?
5. *Making Moral Choices.* – What is my personal moral compass?
6. *Facing Death.* – Confronting the ultimate mystery.
7. *By Whose Authority?* – How do I know what to believe?
8. *Time and History.* – Is there a grand plan for the universe?
9. *The Importance of Belief.* – Is spirituality about believing or about doing?
10. *God.* – Ways of shaping the divine.
11. *Suffering and Evil.* – How can I live in their presence?

The final unit, *A Question of Priorities,* summarises all of the others and brings them together, encouraging you to consider ways in which you might now take what you have gained from this course and apply it your life, so that you can become more spiritually active and whole.

Your group might choose to establish a short simple ritual for the beginning of each session, perhaps the lighting of a chalice or candle, with a short reading or prayer, followed by a few moments for participants to share how they are feeling. You might end each session with another short ritual, marking its closure. You might decide to begin or end with a light meal, perhaps soup, bread, and fruit or cheese.

The rules for the group should be few, but they are important. Members should be punctual. What is said in discussion should remain confidential. No one should feel obliged to contribute to the discussion; it is entirely acceptable to 'pass'. Discussions should be a matter of civilised sharing and gentle debate – not heated argument! Members should listen attentively, with the intention of understanding others' points of view and learning from them.

Participants are asked at times to write down their thoughts and their answers to certain questions. Members of the group might prefer to bring their own notebooks. Or the group leader might simply provide some scrap paper on which members can scribble their notes.

If you get to the end of this course, you will have explored some of the questions that are at the heart of a deepened spiritual awareness. Whatever answers you might have discovered through the process, even if the over-riding answer has been to confirm that you don't have any firm answers, it is hoped that you will have been enriched by your open and honest exploration of those questions.

Unit 1. Your Odyssey

The purpose of this first section is to help you to think about your spiritual journey, to tell your life story, and to reflect on it.

Whatever age you are, whatever your religious background, or lack of one, and whether or not you have ever understood it as such, your life so far has been a spiritual journey, because to be human is to ask questions about the meaning of life, and to wonder. This unit is the next stage of your personal spiritual journey.

Life Spirit is designed so that you can do as many of the individual units as you please, in whatever order you choose. However, ideally you will do this unit first, for two reasons. The first is that it will help everyone in your group to get to know each other better, so that you will be better placed to understand not only *what* they believe but, more importantly, *why* they believe it. The second is that it will help you to understand yourself better as you reflect on the religious and spiritual journey that you are already on.

Someone once said that all theology is autobiography. What that means is that when you reflect on your life and you tell your story, you are also placing your life within a larger context. How you see the world, and the beliefs that you use in order to make sense of the world, are the result of your life experience in that world. If you want to know why someone believes as they do, ask them about their life story.

Take a few moments now to reflect on the history of your religious/ spiritual practice so far, before you are asked to share briefly something about that practice. To help you tell your story, Box 1.1 contains some questions which might serve as your way-marks.

Box 1.1. Your religious background

- What kind of religious upbringing, if any, did you have?
- Have you stayed within the faith of your childhood? Or have you ventured elsewhere? Or have you abandoned organised religion altogether?
- If you did not have a religious upbringing, what has drawn you to consider spiritual questions now?
- Have there been times of particular crisis, celebration, joy, or pain in your life which have challenged your assumptions about what you do or don't believe?

After each person who wishes to do so has shared their story, your group should take a few moments to ask questions or reflect on the members' significant milestones.

Our lives consist of choices

Did you find it revealing to tell the story of your own spiritual journey, and to hear the stories of others? Did you tell your story in chronological order, or did you pick out certain themes and tell it that way?

There are different ways to tell our stories. One way is in terms of the choices we have made. Our lives consist of choices, some of them consciously and deliberately made, others seemingly casual or accidental. Perhaps you have chosen your life's work, or chosen where to live. You may have chosen to share your life with one particular person, and chosen whether or not to participate in a religious community. Some people have the good fortune to be given many choices in life. Others, because of the chances of birth, economy, or opportunity, have fewer options. Sometimes we make choices that seem trivial at the time but which have life-altering consequences. The American poet, Robert Frost, speaks of this in his poem, 'The Road Not Taken'. He describes walking through a wood and having to choose one of two tracks, each leading into the unknown. The poem ends:

Two roads diverged in a wood, and I –
I took the one less traveled by,
And that has made all the difference.

Now you are invited to tell the story of some of the choices that you yourself have made. Box 1.2 suggests some that you might consider.

Box 1.2. Choices you have made

- What was the path that led to your career or your present situation?
- How did you choose where you live?
- How have you chosen to start or end the significant relationships in your life?
- Do you feel that you have been in control of the choices in your life, or does it feel as though choices have been made for you?
- Have you made choices that you now regret?

Some aspects of your life will not have been of your choosing. Things will have happened to you which you did not welcome, which were hard and painful and the cause of grief. But even then, you have had choices. You have had the choice of how to respond to those external events. Have you used them to help you grow in faith and understanding, or have you chosen to be defeated by them? Have you shut yourself down in cynicism and despair?

On the same day, within just an hour of each other, two members of a church congregation died. Both of them died suddenly, painlessly, and for both of them their deaths were the natural conclusion to their long and good lives. The widow of one was saddened, but she soon rallied and re-engaged fully with life, and she accepted gladly and graciously the loving care which the congregation and others gave her through her time of passing sadness. She was thankful for the fifty years of love that she had shared with her husband, and gave thanks for the continuing love of family and her many friends. Her loss did not destroy her. It was part of her continuing spiritual growth and participation in life. It was a joy to be in her company. The other widow responded very differently. She became permanently embittered. She railed against God and the world for having taken away her husband. She abandoned her church community, complaining that the church had let her down, even though she shut the door repeatedly on their many offers of help, and she withdrew too from all other social contact. She spent the rest of her days alone, angry, bitter, and resentful.

In many ways, the external experiences of those two women were the same. Their husbands of many years had died. But one widow used her faith in the intrinsic goodness of life to carry on; indeed, her faith grew richer and deeper through the experience of loss and her response to it. Whereas the other abandoned her faith, which she accused of having failed her, and she collapsed into self-pity. Her heart shrivelled. In effect she died with her husband.

Life is not what happens to us. Life is what we do with what happens to us. We cannot always choose what will happen in life. We can choose how we respond to what happens.

Can you bring to mind any occasions when life has dealt you a hard blow, when something happened which you did not choose or welcome, but which in retrospect was one of the pivotal moments in your spiritual formation? Box 1.3 might help you to identify some such moments.

Box 1.3. How do you respond to life's challenges?

- Think of a sad or challenging event in your life so far. Did you deal with it well? If you are willing, briefly share details with your group.
- Did you grow through that experience, or have you been unable to put down the burden of your grief or frustration?
- What role did your personal faith play in helping you through the experience, and how did the experience affect your faith?

The road ahead

We create our own spirituality as we create our lives. Our spirits are in a state of constant flux and they demand our care. There is no time when our spirits are complete.

The story that you have told is part of the journey of your life so far. But what about the story of our life yet to be? Fortunately, it is not given to us to know our futures. We do not know in advance how long we will live, or the manner of our dying. Yet we live in hope and expectation, not only that we have life still ahead of us, but, more importantly, that our souls will continue to grow. As long as there is life, there is always the potential for spiritual growth. Indeed, there are those who believe in spiritual growth beyond death. Perhaps you are one of them. We will consider that question in another section of this course.

How old are you now? Given reasonable expectations, how much longer do you think you will live? And in that time, what spiritual challenges might you expect to face? Certainly, as we age, we become more aware of mortality, our own and that of those whom we love. Are you spiritually prepared for the challenges of growing older? How will you care for your spirit in the years that await you? Will your spirit age with your body, or will it remain fresh and vital?

If the life that awaits you is anything like the life that you have already had, there will be a share of both the good and the not-so-good. As you have told some of the story of your past life, use the questions in Box 1.4 to ponder what you expect from the life ahead, and how you feel you will respond. What will help you through difficult times that you might endure?

Box 1.4. Facing the future

- How long do you expect to live?
- What do you fear about growing older?
- Are there things that you specifically want to accomplish in your life?
- What measures will you use to evaluate how well you have lived?

We don't often have an opportunity to tell our stories as we have done in this session, or to hear the stories of others. Has it been a rewarding experience, and will you continue on your spiritual journey with other sections in this course?

Ebbs and flows in our spiritual life

For your final discussion on this occasion, can you identify changes in your spirituality, and in how you have needed to express it, over the course of your life? Have there been times when you have actively pursued your spiritual life, and other times when your spiritual life has lain dormant? For example, it is a fairly common phenomenon that people in middle age start to reconnect with their spirituality. They have raised their family, they have achieved whatever financial or material success they might have craved early in their careers, and then they start to wonder, 'Is this it? I have what I thought I wanted, and still I feel empty.'

To conclude this session on telling your spiritual odyssey, use the questions in Box 1.5 to consider such ebbs and flows. You might choose to share your thoughts with other members of the group.

Box 1.5. The life and times of the spirit

• When or why or how has your spirituality been important to you?
• Can you recognise times when you have been spiritually active, and other times when you have been preoccupied with other calls on your energies?
• Think about the times when you have been spiritually active, and the times when you have been spiritually inactive. Can you discern a qualitative difference in how you have felt about your life at those times?

Unit 2. What is spirituality?

The word 'spirituality' is increasingly popular these days. Traditionally, spirituality has been the province of organised religion, but more and more people who reject organised religion are nevertheless keen to explore and develop their spirituality. Go into many churches and you will find empty pews. Go into most bookshops and you will find many shelves filled with books in the Mind/Body/Spirit section. And there is an abundance of conferences, retreats, self-styled gurus and teachers, and courses.

What is going on? Not long ago, most national societies had one dominant faith. In the Western world that faith has been Christianity, and it has dominated all aspects of life, from the national – with laws and social codes and medical ethics based on Christian precepts – to the personal, with individuals basing their own moral code on Christian values, and using Christian language to articulate those values. This had the advantage of underpinning a cohesive social identity. Churches were central to the life of the nation and the local community, and they were the only medium through which spirituality was formally expressed.

There was little or no meaningful communication with cultures and faiths beyond the immediately familiar. Where there were non-Christian faiths, they were practised mainly by marginalised ethnic-minority groups and, whether they were actively oppressed or passively tolerated, those non-Christian faiths did not have any comparable social or political influence on the national identity.

For a variety of reasons, the twentieth century witnessed the crumbling of the central role of the Christian church in public life. The immigration of people of other faiths and traditions, the advance of science and humanist thought which has challenged previously unquestioned assumptions, and the development of communication technologies have all contributed to the church's loss of centrality in national life. And whereas the church once commanded the status of exclusive authority, people now often look elsewhere for their spiritual nourishment, or they look nowhere. There is no single dominant world-view or exclusive way of expressing that world-view. No church, and no priesthood, is any longer the unquestioned authority on all things spiritual.

For some, this decline of organised religion in the Western world has been a good thing. They say that it has freed people from the tyranny of the church. For others it has left a vacuum, with no obvious alternative to fill the void. People have not ceased to be spiritually hungry, but there is no longer just one place at which to satisfy their hunger. They have been left to their own devices, free to choose from the supermarket of spiritualities. And choose they have. Sometimes people make wise choices based on careful thought. Sometimes they make poor choices, and allow themselves to be seduced by questionable cults and sects which may leave them emotionally damaged and financially swindled.

Before you address the question of what spirituality actually is, take some time, using the questions in Box 2.1, to consider or discuss how you view the gradual decline of traditional religion and the diversification of spiritual expression.

Box 2.1. From public religion to private spirituality

- Is the contemporary weakening of traditional religion a good thing?
- What influences do you think have contributed to this shift from the authority of a central church to the freedom of individuals to choose from a supermarket of spiritualities?
- Who or what are the spiritual authorities today?
- What has been gained and what has been lost in the breakdown of spiritual practice?
- Has this shift made us more open to other spiritualities?

Definitions of spirituality

Let's look now more specifically at what spirituality actually is. Many people today describe themselves as spiritual, whether or not they have any active involvement in organised religion. Perhaps you describe yourself as spiritual but not religious. What does that mean? Is it saying anything interesting or profound?

We are all spiritual. To be human is to be spiritual. It is one of the distinguishing features of our humanity that, as far as we know, we are the only species with a spiritual dimension. We are the only species which asks ultimate questions of itself and of life, the only species which worships, and which is self-aware. Spirituality is both the triumph and the curse of our humanity.

What is spirituality? We think we know what it means, but it is not so easy to pin it down. There are many ways in which you could define spirituality. One way of expressing and understanding it is to say that it is our search for and our experience of connection. The search for and experience of connection can take different forms.

Connection with the universe

First, there is our connection with the universe. Have you ever had the experience of standing outside on a beautiful clear night and looking up at the infinite sky and thinking to yourself, 'Wow!'? ('Wow' is one of the most important words in the spiritual vocabulary. 'Wow moments' are moments of intense spiritual experience.) So, you look up at all those stars, and you know that even the closest star is so far away that you can't even begin to comprehend the vastness of what you are looking at. You know that what seems to you vast beyond measure is in fact just a tiny little out-of-the-way corner of only one galaxy, and there are hundreds, even thousands, of galaxies. It can make you feel tiny and insignificant. You know that, since human time began, people have stood and gazed at the stars as you are doing, wondering, marvelling, wanting to make sense of it, weaving it into stories and myths to connect the finite with the infinite.

You might know more than our ancestors about the science of astronomy. You might know, as they did not, that Earth is not the centre of all creation, around which all else moves, but that this Earth is the merest speck of insignificance, compared with all that is. You might know all of that. Yet on this mere speck stands all that is precious to you – everything of love and beauty and significance. You turn your gaze from the heavens to this Earth, and you see nature's beauty and pageantry and complexity. You might not be a creationist in the simplistic fundamentalist sense, but perhaps you are drawn to wonder how all of this came about. How did this miracle of creation happen?

The most magical miracle of all is that life began. How did it begin? Why did it begin? How and why do *you* have life? When you ask such questions, you are delving into the life of your spirit. Because you know that, however small the universe might make you feel, you are part of it: you belong. You are connected to it. You are made of the same physical stuff as all that is. You are, literally, stardust. You are connected with the earth on which you stand; you are connected with the air which you breathe in and out every moment of your life; you are connected with water, without which you could not survive. You are physically connected with everything that you see around you, from the most distant star to the tiniest insect. But, more importantly, you are connected by the invisible bonds of the spirit. Spirituality is the process of seeking and experiencing that intimate connection with the universe of all that is.

Sir Alister Hardy (1896–1985) was a British biologist who became fascinated by such experiences, and he started collecting other people's 'Wow' stories. He studied those stories, he looked for common elements, and he helped people not to feel embarrassed in admitting to having had such experiences. Here is one such story, recorded in Hardy's book, *The Original Vision*.

*I remember instances in my childhood when I felt a unity with the world
around me verging on mystical experience. I did not at first associate
such feelings with religion. They were usually the result of a deep
realisation of beauty in nature or music. They were not so much a sense
of self-consciousness as of absorption in something far greater than myself
of which I was at the same time a part and glad and grateful to be so; an
overwhelming sense of trust and gratitude to the world for letting me be
part of it. This was later amplified and deepened in periods of genuine
spiritual experience when I and the world seemed to dissolve into a new
and vastly more significant reality which had hitherto only been vaguely
sensed but suddenly seemed to be revealed completely, so that one had the
sense that it had always been there but that one had been unaware of it.*

Box 2.2. Connecting with the universe

- Have you had any 'WOW' moments that you are willing to share
  with your group: moments when you have felt connected with the
  universe?
- How do you respond to the beauty of creation?
- What is your spiritual response to the vastness and the timelessness
  of the universe?

If you have addressed the questions in Box 2.2, either alone or in a
group, you have just been grappling with one of the eternal spiritual
questions: how do I fit into the grand scheme and design of all that is?
Am I important to the whole, tiny and ephemeral as I am?

The quest for meaning and purpose

Here is another eternal spiritual question: *What does my life mean?*
Spirituality is not only the quest for connection with the universe. It is
also the quest for connection with meaning and purpose in individual
lives. Like all other forms of life, you were born, you live for a while,
and then you die. That is the eternal circle of life from which none of

us is exempt. But why? What is the point? Is there a point? Perhaps our human life is just a meaningless accident, a bad joke, and the best we can hope for is to get through it with a minimum of suffering and discomfort, and when we die that is the end. Or is there some grander scheme, some nobler end than an inevitable return to the dust?

One function of spirituality is to address that larger quest for connection with meaning and purpose which places the individual within the context of a grander vision. Some of those answers might seem fanciful to the sophisticated modern mind, but even the most modern mind craves a context. Knowing that you are going to die, how are you to live so that your death does not deny your life's meaning? Spirituality is seeking connection with purpose beyond self, with that which will not die with you. Many people, having acquired financial or worldly success, discover with dismay that such success gives them little satisfaction. Their life still feels hollow to them, because they have not connected with a larger purpose beyond themselves. Spirituality is the connection of the individual self with meaning and purpose beyond self.

That purpose must involve ethical living. Spirituality is also connection with ethical living.

The quest for ethical living

Most of us have a sense of right and wrong. We want to live with integrity and authenticity. We want an ethical code. We want it not only for our own benefit but because we want our lives to touch those of others. Some people distort personal spirituality into an exclusive focus on themselves. They think that it is all about them, that the only thing which matters is that they attain some imagined paradise, and it does not matter what happens to others. The *Life Spirit* course offers very few absolutes. But here is one: if your spirituality is only about you and the state of your soul, so that you have no regard for the physical or spiritual well-being of others, then your spirituality is worthless. It is a corruption. Authentic spirituality is about living in right relationship with others – all others –

in ways which contribute to their good as much as they do to your own. Every great spiritual teacher has said the same, if in slightly different forms. Do unto others as you would have them do unto you.

Spirituality is the search for connection with meaning and purpose, and connection with ethical living. Box 2.3 offers some questions for you to consider.

Box 2.3. Connecting with meaning

- Does life have meaning?
- What gives meaning to your life?
- Is there tension between your answers to the first and second questions?
- Is it possible to have a meaningful life in isolation from other people?

If you are following this course in a group, did you all reach a consensus in response to those questions about meaning, purpose, and ethical living – or could you not agree?

Cultivating spirituality

There is one other very important aspect of spirituality. Spirituality is partly a matter of practice. Some people think that spiritual experience is just something which happens. It is certainly true that moments of heightened spiritual awareness can and do happen spontaneously, and many people have testified to having such experiences. At such times they feel absolutely at peace, absolutely reassured about their oneness with everything. At such moments of spiritual intensity, time loses its meaning. Such is the true meaning of eternal life: not living for ever, but life beyond time; life lived as if time did not matter; life measured by quality and intensity, not quantity.

Such moments of spiritual ecstasy are real, and they can and do come unbidden. However, spirituality is also a discipline. We might all have a spiritual dimension, but that dimension requires work if it is to be healthy and flourish. We have a physical dimension, but our physicality needs a good diet and regular exercise in order to be healthy. If we want our bodies to be able to do things, we have to keep them in good shape. We have an intellectual dimension, but our brains also need regular exercise. It is the same with our spirits.

Our spirits must be used. They must be kept active and in good shape. Spirituality is about ritual, the repetition of practice, and observance of that which will keep us healthy.

Even when you might not at first want to tend to your spirit, the act of doing so anyway is the ritual. Writers say that the most important element in being a successful writer is to write. That is, sit down at your desk and write. Have a routine and stick to it. Those who await inspiration before they write anything end up not writing anything at all. Athletes know that they must train, even when they might not want to, if they are to achieve their goals of athletic success. Top athletes don't say, 'Oh, I just train when I feel like it'. They train because they know they must. Musicians, however great their native talent, have to practise. Indeed, the greater their talent, the harder they practise. And the better they get, the harder still do they practise. There is the theory of 10,000 hours: whatever the field – music or sport or academic research or even spirituality – those who are truly great are those who have done at least 10,000 hours of practice. Native talent is all very well, but native talent without 10,000 hours does not amount to success in your chosen pursuit.

How many hours have you devoted to the care of your soul? If you want to be spiritually healthy, you need to practise your spirituality. You can choose what your practice will be, but, having chosen it, you have to do it. For some, it might be regular church-going, even on those Sunday mornings when they really would prefer to lie in bed or go to the garden centre. For others, it might be meditation, chanting, yoga, t'ai chi – you name it. *What* it is, is less important than *that* it is, and that you do it.

Spirituality is not only about connection – with the universe, with meaning and purpose, and with ethical living: it is the repeated intentional engagement with that which creates and facilitates that connection.

The questions in Box 2.4 might help you to consider and discuss your own spiritual disciplines and practices.

Box 2.4. Connecting with practice

- Do you agree that spirituality requires practice?
- What practices do you already do?
- What have you tried which did not work for you?
- What might you like to try?
- What benefit would you hope to derive from such new practices?

Unit 3. The role of personal faith

In Unit 2, we explored the idea that spirituality means seeking and experiencing connection – with the universe, with meaning and purpose, and with ethical living – and we concluded with a preliminary look at the concept of spiritual practice. In this unit we will take further our investigation into what having a personal faith means.

Many people think that faith is about subscribing to beliefs. If you tell them that you are a person of faith, their likely response is to ask something like: 'What do you believe about x, y, or z?' Unless, of course, you belong to a well-known faith, let's say Catholicism, in which case people assume that you believe what the church tells you to believe. This is particularly likely in the Western world, still dominated by Christianity. Very early in its development, Christianity came to define itself according to correct belief. The original followers of Jesus had not thought of themselves like that. They called themselves 'People of the Way', following the path of life set for them by Jesus. However, as those early disciples grappled with some of the theological mysteries of their faith, and as they tried to explain those mysteries to potential converts, they got sidetracked from following a way of life into arguing about beliefs.

Faith or dogma?

Early Christianity became an intellectual religion, with theologians writing lengthy treatises, and official doctrine being decided by Councils not unlike present-day political-party conferences deciding upon manifestos. The most famous of those Councils was held in Nicaea, in the year 325 AD. It had been convened by the Roman emperor Constantine the Great, who wanted to exert his control over Christianity, to which he had nominally converted. Constantine was interested in political domination, not theological speculation. Nevertheless, he brought together all the bishops and insisted that they come up with a statement. It took weeks of debate and political manoeuvring, but what was finally decided at Nicaea, almost 1,700 years ago, became known as the Nicene Creed. Ever since, the reciting of that creed has been the bedrock of Christian liturgy.

What does the Nicene Creed say? In its slightly revised form, dating from 381, it begins:

> *I believe in One God, the Father Almighty, Maker of Heaven and Earth, and in one Lord Jesus Christ, the only-begotten son of God...*

And so it goes on. Perhaps you can recite it by heart, so often have you said it as an integral part of your worship Sunday by Sunday. Or perhaps you have never heard it before, and are puzzled by what relevance it could possibly have for today's modern, rational world. But note: it begins with the words, *I believe...*

However, it may be that many people who recite that creed, Sunday by Sunday, don't actually believe it. For most, reciting the Creed is not a way to state their beliefs, but a way to participate in the community of the faithful, to identify with the long tradition of the Christian church. It is none the worse for that. The point of reciting the Creed, for those who do, is not necessarily the literal meaning of the words, which for many have long since lost their power; it is the comfort of repetition, the ritual act of declaring that this is the religious community to which you belong.

Nevertheless, the Nicene Creed, if taken literally, does ask you to believe some things which challenge today's rational mind. Some people think that the role of faith is to make you believe things which you would not or could not believe otherwise: that faith is the willing suspension of rational, critical thought. One of the early Christian theologians, trying to explain the Trinity and getting himself into a terrible tangle, finally exclaimed, 'It is impossible. That is why I believe it.'

Human reason certainly does not have the answers to all questions, and it never will. Indeed, at the heart of spiritual faith there always remains acceptance of mystery beyond reason. But the point of faith is not to believe the unbelievable. The point of faith is to use human reason to its fullest capacity, but then to find contentment and assurance within inexplicable, ineffable mystery.

An article of faith

In Unit 9 we explore the role of belief in greater detail. But for now, write down a brief statement which begins with the words *'I believe...'*. It does not have to be a statement of the bedrock of your belief. Write down just one thing that you believe is true, and to which you give not only intellectual assent but your heart. A belief, in other words, which is important to you and helps to govern your life.

For example, you may believe in the invincibility of human goodness. This means that no matter what evil might prevail, human goodness can never be wholly eradicated. It is a belief which fills you with hope when you would otherwise despair, and it is a belief which prevents you from surrendering to cynicism. It is a belief that cannot be proven. It is a belief held in the face of plenty of evidence to the contrary. In other words, ultimately it is a belief that is an article of faith.

Box 3.1. An article of faith

- Can you provide a single statement of your own belief?
- Why do you hold that belief?
- Why it is important to you?

If you are happy to do so, now share your article of faith with your group. Then take time to discuss your collected statements. What kinds of statement did your group come up with? Does your group hold a wide diversity of actual beliefs, or is there considerable agreement among you?

Faith as a way of seeing the world

Beliefs are important. They form the intellectual framework within which we live and move and have our being. But ultimately faith is not about holding particular beliefs. Two people can stand side by side and each can recite the same creed with full conviction, and yet they can have very different understandings and experiences of what their faith means to them. Ultimately faith goes beyond language or thought. Faith is about the way we see the world. Is the world fundamentally rich with meaning and wonder, or is it empty and pointless?

The story of the Sky Maiden

In West Africa the people of a certain tribe noticed that their cows gave less milk than in the past. The cows seemed as healthy as before, but each morning they produced less milk. Finally one young man offered to stay up all night to see if anything strange was happening. He hid behind some bushes, and after a while was astonished to see a beautiful maiden come down to Earth on a moonbeam. She carried a pail with her, and silently she milked the cows before ascending back to the sky on another moonbeam. The man could scarcely believe his eyes, so the next night he lay in hiding again and, sure enough, down came the Sky Maiden once more with her pail, and silently she milked the cows before returning to the sky. The third night he lay in wait again, but this time he set a trap, and when the Sky Maiden descended he sprang the trap and caught her.

'*Please let me go,*' pleaded the beautiful maiden.

'*First tell me who you are.*'

So she explained that she came from a tribe who lived in the sky, where they had no food of their own. It was her task to descend to Earth each night to collect food for her tribe. Without her, her people would starve. But the young man had fallen in love with her great beauty, and he refused to set her free. Instead, he demanded that she marry him.

'I will marry you,' she relented, *'but first you must allow me to return to my people. I promise I will return in three days.'*

The man agreed, and the maiden rode a moonbeam back to the sky. True to her word, in three days' time she returned, this time bringing with her a box.

'I will marry you,' said the Sky Maiden, *'but you must promise me you will never look inside the box.'*

He gave his word, and they married. At first they were very happy, but in time the man grew curious about what might be hidden in the box. So one day, when his wife was out, he opened the lid. The box was empty. Puzzled, he closed the lid and awaited his wife's return. As soon as she saw him, she knew.

'You have opened the box, haven't you?', she said. *'I must leave you.'*

'Why?', he demanded. *'What is so wrong about looking inside an empty box?'*

'I am not leaving you because you opened the box', she replied. *'I am leaving you because you said it was empty. It was not empty. It was full of sky. When I returned to my home before we married, I filled it with everything that was most precious to me. How can I live with you, when all that is precious to me is mere emptiness to you?'*

Faith as ultimate trust

When people look at the world, they can have very different responses, although they see the same thing. Some seem to see nothing but emptiness. They see human greed and folly. They see war, cynicism, despair, and selfishness. Others look at the same world and they see fullness, generosity and kindness, determination, and steadfast loyalty. Each viewpoint is a position of faith. What do you see? What do you choose to see?

Faith is the way in which you see the world. Is the world a place of hopefulness for you, or a place of despair? Is it a place of beauty, or a place of ugliness? Is it a place worthy of ultimate trust, or do you treat it with guarded suspicion?

You can develop beliefs which codify and articulate that fundamental view of the world. But the beliefs follow on from the primary position of faith and trust. Whatever your ultimate faith, it will be given expression in your beliefs. Spend some time now exploring how you see the world. Use the questions in Box 3.2 to guide you.

Box 3.2. Ways of seeing the world

- Is the world rich or poor?
- Can you identify reasons why you see the world as either a place of emptiness or a place of fullness?
- Are some ways of seeing the world better than others?
- What things give you ultimate hope?

How was your discussion? Did you find that your group consisted essentially of 'half-full' people, or 'half-empty' people?

Faith in action

Consider now what faith means in terms of your daily life. Faith is not only an internalised experience of how you see the world and how you form beliefs which express that view. It is also about how you conduct yourself in the world and in your relationships with other people. Are you a person of compassion and goodness, or a person of ill-will and cruelty? A faith which does not translate into deeds in your daily life in harmony with the ideals that you profess is hollow and hypocritical.

Some deeds of faith might be directly aimed at changing the world. Many people feel compelled by their faith to be directly involved in working for social justice, alleviating the suffering of others, campaigning for peace, protecting the environment, working in education and health and the political process. Others, equally faithful, prefer a more intimate sphere for their deeds. They perform simple acts of kindness to neighbours, and they are the unnoticed leaven in local communities.

Think of someone whom you admire whose faith is or was expressed in their life. It might be someone famous – for example, Mother Theresa, Bishop Desmond Tutu, Martin Luther King Jr – or it might be someone whom you know personally in your own life. And when you have identified the person, consider the questions in Box 3.3.

Box 3.3. A person of faith

- What do you admire about this person?
- How are that person's actions consistent with his or her personal faith?
- Do you discern inconsistencies in that person, and do those inconsistencies add to or detract from their overall impact as a person of faith?
- Would you like to be more like him or her, and, if so, how would you need to change?

Unit 4. The role of organised religion

In Unit 2 we explored the question of what spirituality is, and in Unit 3 we looked at the role of personal faith. In this session we will consider the role of organised religion.

It can be argued that organised religion, in all of its many forms and in spite of its many imperfections, is the best vehicle for the spiritual nurture of individuals, and that it has made and continues to make an enormous contribution to the improvement of society.

However, the story of organised religion is not always a happy one. It is difficult to justify the terrible barbarity of the medieval crusades, for example. But although religion has sometimes been the primary cause of conflict and terrible cruelty, more often than not it has been a convenient rallying cry for other causes – political, economic, or personal. The Catholics and Protestants of Northern Ireland did not fight each other for thirty bitter years over the finer points of Christian doctrine. Religion was just a convenient way to differentiate between the two sides, with each side invoking their religious allegiance as justification for their partisan struggle. The real cause was the underclass, who happened to be primarily Catholic, rising up against centuries of political oppression and economic injustice imposed by the ruling class, which happened to be primarily Protestant.

Although it has undoubtedly been used to fuel war and conflict, and it is true that religious conviction can too easily be corrupted into hateful bigotry, religion itself has also contributed a great deal to human civilisation. There would hardly have been any art in the Western world had it not been for the inspiration of Christianity. No music, no visual art, no literature, no architecture, no scholarship. And what is true of the Western world is equally true of every other culture and civilisation. Whether it be Islam or

Buddhism, Hinduism or the Tao, organised religion has been one of the great inspirations for human imagination and creativity, and one of the great patrons of individual artists. The language and imagery of scripture and sacred ritual often form the bedrock of a society's collective creative consciousness. They certainly do in the Western world.

It is true that religions tend to be conservative. But while that conservatism can sometimes suppress human creativity, it has also often been the institutional foil against which individual creativity arises, and the conservatism validates and authenticates that which has been created. Usually, the dynamic is that a creative individual, or group of individuals, challenges the status quo from within the stability of the organisation, and slowly, through dialogue and compromise and the force of argument, change is effected. If religions were not institutionally conservative, they would be at the mercy of every passing fashion, and essential connection with what is valuable from the community of the past would be jeopardised.

Many people who fully recognise the faults and limitations of organised religions of all kinds continue to believe in their value. Many have been nurtured and encouraged by it throughout their lives. However, that is not everyone's experience. Some people come to an awareness of their spirituality without any previous experience of religion – and some people have been badly hurt by religion. Before you proceed further with this examination of religion, and the role that it plays in spirituality, it would be good to have a conversation about your experiences. Use the questions in Box 4.1 as a guide.

Box 4.1. Organised religion: good or bad?

- Have you had a good or a bad experience of organised religion?
- Are you basically in favour of religion, or do you think it is pernicious?
- If you are neither wholly for nor wholly against religion, what do you see as its good points and its bad points?

Context, form, and continuity

One thing that organised religion does is provide context and form. It gives shape and direction to the individual's personal spiritual journey. Very few of us would be able to invent our own religious beliefs or practices if left solely to our own devices. Organised religion provides a community of identity which reaches back to the traditions of past generations and forwards to the future. That continuity is essential, even if it is in constant evolution and change. Indeed, there is always evolution and change, even in those religions that try to adhere most tenaciously to the traditions of the past. A religion might proclaim a truth as eternal, but its interpretation of that eternal truth is always subject to the passing influences of the time.

Religion is not only about a community of the past, it also creates a community of today. The very word comes from the Latin word *religio*, meaning a bond. That has a double meaning. Religion binds people to each other, bringing them into community. And it binds the individual person into a sense of their own wholeness.

A question of identity

In the first sense, religion forms the common basis of a shared identity. People often say something apparently trite, such as 'Manchester United is my religion'. Actually, being an ardent fan of a football club is much like belonging to a religion. You gather in the holy space of your team's stadium with other people who share your devotion, and there are rituals to learn and repeat together. You dress in the same way, wearing your team's strip, which identifies your loyalty. You go for a drink beforehand, have a meat pie at half-time, and another couple of pints and a kebab on the way home as you glory in your team's success, or indulge the sorrows of your disappointment but console yourself with the hope that things will be different at the next game.

Being a keen supporter of a football team satisfies many of the basic human needs that for others are fulfilled by their religious faith. It gives shape and form to an important part of your life. You know where you have to be at a certain time, you know who will be there with you, and what you will do when you are there. You know the chants and the songs, the personalities and the myths. In other words, it is about much more than football. It is about belonging, about being part of the collective story, not only observing the story but helping to create it. In his book entitled *Fever Pitch* (1992), the novelist Nick Hornby, himself a devoted fan of Arsenal Football Club, both celebrates and bemoans the obsessive hold that being a football fan has on him.

Belonging to an organised religion is much the same. You know where you have to be at a certain time, and who will be there with you, and what you will do when you are there. You know what to wear and where to sit, you know the chants and the songs and the customs, which seem perfectly natural to you because they are your customs and you have been doing them for a long time without ever questioning why, but which can seem completely mystifying to someone seeing them for the first time. You know the stories that will be told, the rituals that will be re-enacted, and you know that next week you will do the same thing again. It is about much more than what is actually happening in a service of worship in terms of the sermon and the prayers and the hymns. It is about belonging, about being part of the collective story, not only observing the story but helping to create the story. *Being the story.*

Use the questions in Box 4.2 to consider what church-goers might learn from football fans about the need to belong to a self-defining community.

Box 4.2. The need to belong

- What are the benefits and disadvantages of being a committed sports fan?
- What are the benefits and disadvantages of being a committed church-goer?
- What similarities and differences are there between attending church and following a sport such as football?

One thing that is sometimes required of someone who wishes to belong to any community is animosity towards those who belong elsewhere. The intention is to achieve clarity of self-definition. The greatest rivalries between football fans are usually between those of neighbouring clubs. Local derbies have their own special intensity. The same is often true in religion. The bitterest sectarian disputes often occur between those who used to be united, just as family fights are often the most vicious. To emphasise their own religious identity, people sometimes feel compelled to vilify the identity of others.

Even for those who do not do this, there is a real sense in which the customs and rituals of an organised religion can seem strange, even alien, to those who don't belong. And that very strangeness can serve as a positive mark of separate identity for the people who do subscribe to those customs and rituals. Moreover, belonging comes at the price of learning the customs and rituals. Religion is an accumulation of rituals, stories, behaviours, customs, and beliefs which are the collective property of all who fall within its compass.

Consider the rituals associated with a concert of classical music. Members of the orchestra come in, all immaculately dressed in black. Then the violinist on the first stand gets up, and the oboist plays a note which the other musicians use to tune their instruments. Then the leader of the orchestra walks on stage and takes a bow while the audience applauds. Finally on comes the conductor, who bows and then addresses the orchestra, and then they start to play. But be warned: don't applaud between movements! How often does a newcomer to classical music make that mistake?

All groups and communities have their own rituals which you have to learn in order to join. One feature of those rituals is that the people who do them usually don't even recognise them as rituals. They think that is just the way in which things are done.

Box 4.3. The role of ritual

Think of a group to which you belong, or an activity that you regularly do, and identify rituals and modes of behaviour of that group or that activity.

- Does it involve a dress code?
- Do you have certain ways to address each other?
- How did you learn the rituals?
- How do you teach them to newcomers?

Recall a situation in which you were a visitor and there were rituals and practices which everyone else seemed to know and understand, but you had no idea what was going on. It might have attendance at a place of worship, or it might have been a concert or a social situation.

- Can you identify what those practices were?
- Did they seem strange?
- How did you – if at all – learn those practices?

The individual and the church

Not only do the rituals and practices of organised religion serve to bind people to each other; they are also the instruments through which the individuals bind themselves into a coherent scheme of self-understanding. They enable us to develop our strengths and also come to terms with our failings. They provide the context within which we seek self-improvement and self-forgiveness, and they offer the hope of a fulfilling destiny. They seek to convince us that we are of value. At their best, they bring mind, body, and spirit into one, binding the individual into the cohesive whole.

Being a human invention, organised religion is only as good as the people who comprise it. It is as vulnerable to human corruption, folly, and incompetence as any other human creation. But it is also the

33

institutional guardian of the human quest for spirituality. For all its weakness, religion is what makes spirituality possible. An individual can be spiritual without participating in organised religion, although that is difficult; but when two or three are gathered together to explore their spirituality, there is religion. Even doing this course, which you might have chosen to do because you want to explore and develop your personal spirituality, means that you are working within the context of a group of other people, and your own group will have developed its own rituals and habits already. For example, have you sat in the same chair each time? Do you have refreshments, and have you established how you do that, so that people now just know what the routine is?

Box 4.4 offers some final questions for you to consider.

Box 4.4. In the final analysis ...

- Do you think the world would be a better place if there were no organised religion? Or is the existence of organised religion an inevitable manifestation of the essential human need to explore and give collective expression to the fact of our spirituality?
- Could you be spiritual all by yourself?
- Has your understanding of religion changed as a result of this unit?

Unit 5. Making moral choices

One of the most important defining characteristics of being human is that we make choices. We have free will. And because it is an essential part of our humanity, it is also what leads us into a lot of trouble and difficulty, because we often choose badly. We choose things which cause pain to ourselves or to others. We choose from the wrong motives – of greed, or vanity, or selfishness – rather than from motives of love or kindness or decency. However, although we often abuse it, the freedom to choose is essential to our full humanity.

This aspect of the human condition is dramatically illustrated by the story of Adam and Eve, as told in the Bible in the Book of Genesis. This story is a myth. In popular parlance, 'myth' has come to mean a lie or a deception, something which is not true. However, myths are very important in spiritual traditions. A myth is a story which may or may not be historically factual, and very often isn't, but its importance is in the truth that it conveys about the human condition. The genius of the story of Adam and Eve is that it speaks to what is essential to being fully human, namely the ability to discern between good and evil, to make choices which have consequences, and then to suffer those consequences.

The story is a familiar one. Adam and Eve occupy the Garden of Eden, living in a state of innocence, and all is well with the world. There is only one thing that they are told they must not do: they must not eat the fruit of the Tree of the Knowledge of Good and Evil. Now Adam and Eve were like all children since: tell them not to do something and, sure enough, sooner or later they are going to do it. You know how it is, even as an adult. You see a sign saying Wet Paint, and you just have to touch it. And Adam and Eve can't resist the temptation: they do eat the forbidden fruit, and it is only then that they learn what is right and wrong. For the first time they feel shame and guilt. They lose their state of child-like innocence. The thing that makes us fully responsible as adults is the very thing that destroys our innocence as children.

The same theme is explored in many other myths and legends. For example, the story of the child-man Enkidu in the epic of Gilgamesh, the greatest surviving work of early Mesopotamian culture. It is even explored in the story of the twentieth-century American comic hero, Superman, who falls in love with Lois Lane and loses his superhuman powers when he consummates that love. The theme is consistent: to become fully human is to fall from the grace of innocence.

Yet, who of us would wish to remain in a state of perpetual innocence if it were to mean that we were never to grow up? Who of us would want to be Peter Pan, forever a child, forever irresponsible? Is there not something pathetic about the adult child who has never taken responsibility for himself or herself, who remains arrested in a state of childish dependency, unfulfilled as an authentic adult?

The study of Moral Philosophy explores this idea by posing the existence of a drug called the Happy Drug. Those who took it would be in a state of permanent happiness. They would simply lie down on a bed and enjoy uninterrupted bliss for the rest of their lives. Other people would feed them, bathe them, nurse them. The question is this: would you take the drug? If not, why not? Even though it would guarantee your happiness, it would be at the cost of surrendering something elemental about who you are or who you want to be as a person. You are an adult. As such, you are a person who makes choices, and who is held responsible for those choices. Which of us, had we been in the Garden of Eden, would not have eaten the fruit of the Tree of the Knowledge of Good and Evil? That is the universal power of the story. It nails us. We choose to know the difference between good and evil, even though we know it will bring us pain. As humans we demand the right to choose. Anything less, and we know we would be less than fully human.

Now spend some time exploring the story of Adam and Eve in the Garden of Eden. Please resist the temptation to argue whether the story is historically factual. That is not important. The story's truth lies in what it says about who we are. Whether or not it actually happened is as irrelevant as it is uninteresting. Box 5.1 offers some questions that you might want to consider.

Box 5.1. Adam and Eve: the archetypal story of Free Will

- Was Adam and Eve's sin disobedience, or was it the inevitable need to fulfil their humanity?
- Would you want to live in a state of morality-free innocence if it meant surrendering the ability to make your own choices?
- Is the knowledge of Good and Evil the defining point of adult humanity?
- Do you know other stories and myths which have the same theme as the story of Adam and Eve?

External authority or individual discernment?

As humans we make choices. Let us assume that we want to make good choices. In any given situation, how do we know what the correct moral choice is? And what is the role of our spirituality in guiding those choices?

You might follow a particular teacher, or a spiritual path which is very directive in its moral guidance. It might lay down clear rules of behaviours and attitudes. For example, some forms of Buddhist and Hindu teachings specifically prohibit the eating of meat. Buddhists and Hindus are vegetarians therefore not for reasons of physical health or agricultural economy or political conviction, but because it forms an integral part of their spiritual discipline as prescribed by their chosen teacher. On the other hand, vegetarians in our modern Western society might have made that commitment as a personal moral choice, having weighed up the issue on whatever grounds are important to them – economic sustainability, animal welfare, or personal health. The former have chosen to follow another's directive. The latter have chosen through their own discernment.

So if you have a spiritual and moral mentor, Jesus or the Buddha or whoever it might be, and you have studied that person's teachings and you have chosen to follow that teacher's path in all circumstances, then your spirituality has a direct bearing on how you will behave, and what choices you will make. Your morality is a direct product of your spirituality. Doing it that way certainly makes things more straightforward. Note: straightforward, not easy. Morality is never easy. As a disciple you would say, 'What does my teacher require of me in this situation?', and the answer to that question would tell you what to do. Perhaps there is a book of instructions written by the teacher. Or perhaps the moral code will be the collected interpretations of subsequent scholars and priests.

However, if you do not identify with a particular religious tradition which offers specific moral instruction, then you are far more dependent on your own powers of discernment. Instead of saying, 'This is right because my spiritual teacher says it is right', you have to use other criteria for determining how to act. What criteria might they be?

Definitions of morality

Let's assume that you are not a sociopath and you want to do what is good and right. The questions still remain: 'What is the good? How will you define what is good?'

Let's look at one moral dilemma as an example: the issue of abortion. Assume that everyone involved in this dilemma is a person of high principle and moral rectitude, acting with the best of intentions. Still, there will be many different points of view. One person might assert that the foetus is already a living entity, that its soul is already in place, and the fact that it has not yet emerged from the womb is not a relevant moral factor. Therefore, to deliberately end that life is no different from deliberately ending the life of a person who has been born. In other words, abortion is murder, which must in all cases be opposed, and anyone who participates in abortion, whether as the mother or as a member of the medical profession, is guilty of murder, even in circumstances of rape or direct danger to the life or health of the mother. That is an absolutist position and it is a legitimate point of view.

However, if you regard abortion as the taking of life, and you have an absolute prohibition against taking another life, does that extend to capital punishment? Does it extend to taking life in a just war, or even in self-defence? Is it permissible to be an absolutist only when it suits you?

Another person might take the absolutist view on abortion at the other end of the spectrum, insisting that the question of abortion should be the decision of the mother alone. This argument, which has larger implications for sexual politics, maintains that a woman must have autonomy over what happens to her body, and it is nobody else's business. But does everyone have an absolute right to do with their body whatever they wish? Are we not each members of a larger society to which we owe some legal and moral obligation? If you claim that a woman has an absolute right to abort her unborn child, would you defend a woman who is eight months pregnant with a healthy foetus and decides to abort because she had just been invited to go on a beach holiday and wants to look good in her bikini?

A third person might adopt a more consequential moral code in deciding what to do in the case of abortion, wanting to judge each individual case on its own merits. Factors which can be brought into consideration might include the social and economic circumstances into which the child would be born, the threat posed by the pregnancy to the life or well-being of the mother, and the circumstances of the conception – was it a case of rape, or incest? That third person would take all those factors into consideration, and make a decision about that particular situation. Such a situational moral code has the advantage of being responsive to the circumstances of each case, but it suffers from a lack of clarity and consistency. If each case is different, on what basis do you make your moral decisions? And with such subjective relativism, is it ever right or even possible to impose one person's judgement on someone else?

Those are three different moral positions on the same issue. Each of them can be adopted by persons of honour and moral probity. Using abortion as a case where moral choices have to be made, consider your own position. More importantly, try to identify your general moral stance. Use the questions in Box 5.2 as a guide.

Box 5.2 What is the basis of your own morality?

- Do you believe that there are moral absolutes, to be invoked and applied in all circumstances?
- Are you a moral relativist, trying to weigh up the costs and benefits in each situation?
- Are you a utilitarian, believing in whatever promotes the greatest good for the greatest number?
- What is your moral compass?

The motives behind the morals

There is not only the moral question of right and wrong choices; there is also the moral question of right and wrong motivations. Beneath every moral choice there lies a complex web of motivations – legal, social, psychological, and even theological.

Fear of punishment for making the wrong choice might prevail in your decision. If you believe in a supreme God who judges you and who will hold you ultimately accountable for your choices, you are likely to make your choices with that factor very much in mind. Another factor might be your social standing, and the need to appear upright and respectable and to enjoy society's approval. In that case, your greatest punishment would be the shame that you would feel if you were found out.

Action and motivation are not necessarily always consistent. It is possible to do the right thing for the wrong reason, and the wrong thing for the right reason. How do we discern and judge? Do you judge morality primarily according to motive, or according to action? Is the definition of 'good' that which is done, or that which was meant? And how can we be sure of motives, our own and those of others, when it is possible to do the same action from noble motives or from base motives?

Theologians and moral philosophers have been arguing about these questions for centuries. There are many different schools of thought which offer definitions and prescribe codes of conduct. A practical spirituality requires not only that we develop an intellectual framework of beliefs about the world, and not only that we are attentive to the rituals and customs that nurture our spirituality. It also requires that we live out our faith in the world of human interaction and relationship. How we treat others is evidence of our personal spirituality.

Box 5.3 contains some questions for your concluding consideration or discussion.

Box 5.3. Motivation and conscience

- Describe a time when you have done something and your motives have been misconstrued – by yourself or by others.
- Is morality primarily determined by the action itself, or by the motivation for the action?
- Consider the concept of 'conscience'. What is it? How is it informed by the larger communities of which you are part: by religion, by your particular social set, or by society in general?
- Do you behave morally for the intrinsic value of doing so, or because you fear the consequences of not doing so?

Unit 6. Facing death

This unit will examine life's greatest mystery: death. The one absolutely certain thing that we know about every individual life is that it must eventually end. That is the universal condition for all living creatures. There are no exceptions. You can't argue or bargain your way out of it.

This is not a particularly palatable fact. Death is a subject which many of us find difficult to talk about. Most of us, most of the time, quite like living, and we want to keep on doing it for as long as possible. Those who choose not to keep on living, who prefer to end their lives for whatever reason, are usually regarded with fear or suspicion or disapproval by the rest of us, because their choosing to die challenges our cherished assumptions about life and its value and importance.

Religion, in many ways, is the human response to the twin realities that we are alive and that we have to die. Other species might know that they must die, and their instincts are usually for survival; but, as far as we know, we are the only species which has the self-awareness to reflect on this twin reality of knowing that we are alive and knowing that we must die. It is both the triumph and the tragedy of the human condition to be able to ponder on our own mortality. Out of that has arisen religion, the attempt to explain, to justify, or to mitigate the pain of the knowledge that we must die.

Religious attempts to make sense of death

Religion has tried to answer this great imponderable in many different ways. One thing common to all the world's major religions, and the minor ones, is that they have a meta-narrative which tries to make sense of death, to frame it in a larger context, to remove its sting. A meta-narrative is the story which underpins a system of belief.

One such meta-narrative which some religions have developed to mitigate the pain of death has been to deny its reality. In other words, some say, death is only the threshold to another (better) world, or the opportunity to re-enter this world in a different form. One way of doing this is to separate the body, which manifestly and incontrovertibly does die, from the soul, which for a time is housed (or trapped) in the physical body but which survives beyond death and is a person's eternal essence. This meta-narrative, found in different forms in Christianity, Islam, and Judaism, says that this life is merely the ante-chamber to another, more abiding, life, the quality and location of which are determined by the quality of this earthly life. There are things we can do in this life, and beliefs we can hold, which will decide whether we shall enter into that eternal life of bliss. The purpose of religion, therefore, is to provide the necessary practical and spiritual guidance to ensure our safe passage to that awaiting paradise. In this meta-narrative, each individual soul is a one-off unique phenomenon, precious in the sight of God, for which there is an eternal destiny of either salvation or damnation.

Other religious meta-narratives, found more usually in Eastern traditions, regard the human soul not as living once upon this Earth in a uniquely precious human manifestation, but as engaged in a revolving process to perfection. This meta-narrative says that the soul repeatedly returns to Earth in different forms, for the purpose of learning and growing until it has become sufficiently mature and divine to be able to escape this world and enter into a state of spiritual wholeness which no longer requires the physical form.

In more recent times, particularly in the Western world, there has been a rise in a third alternative: a kind of scientific pragmatism which says that death is the end of our human consciousness, and that there is no after-life of any kind. This is not necessarily nihilistic. Such a view does not have to mean an absence of spirituality. It does mean a spirituality based on this life for its own sake, rather than this life as preparation for something else.

Given those three broad views of what happens when we die, which do you favour? Box 6.1 contains some questions that you might like to keep in mind during your conversation.

Box 6.1. Personal perspectives on death

- Is this life a once-only preparation for eternal life?
- Is this life one episode in a series of lives which will lead to eventual release from this world?
- Is this life all there is, and is death the end of all personal consciousness?
- What are your reasons for believing as you do? Or are your beliefs based on wishful thinking?
- Do you have any direct experience which has led you to your beliefs?

Whichever of those three broad views of death you find most appealing or plausible, the only thing we know for certain about death is that we do not know for certain what happens after we die. It is all speculation. You should be wary of anyone who claims to have the definitive answer to this question. How do they know?

An alternative perspective

Here is one prism through which to view this puzzle. One thing that we learn from science is that energy and matter can't be destroyed: we can only change them into other forms. If that is true of our physical selves, might it also be true of our non-physical selves? Might it be that spiritual energy or matter can't be destroyed either?

Consider this. Suppose you eat an apple. You digest the nutrients of that apple, and they are distributed throughout your body to give you strength, to heal damaged tissues, to grow hair and fingernails and skin, to perform a host of complicated and intricate biological functions. In a real sense, the apple becomes you. And then your body discharges what it does not need, and that discharge returns to the earth, and from that earth grows a new apple tree. And so the cycle continues. Each individual atom is at one time an apple, and then you, and then who knows what. Nothing is new. Everything is recycled.

Does that also apply to our non-physical selves? Is it equally impossible to destroy emotional or spiritual energy, and instead does it just change into different forms? Might it be that our spirits, whatever they are, are fluid and in constant flux and are not the exclusive one-time property of ourselves, but interchangeable with other manifestations of spiritual energy? Actually, one cannot separate the physical from the non-physical. The apple not only feeds your body, it also gives you energy to think and feel and love, to worship and to pray. In other words, the apple feeds your spirit as well as your body. Therefore, your soul, whatever soul is, abides for ever. But in what form? Does it live for ever as a single separate entity, or as a constantly changing part of an undifferentiated whole?

Ultimately we cannot know. All we can know is that in this life we must die. And facing that fact challenges how we shall live. Whereas some people find the prospect of their own death appalling, others find the prospect of living for ever even more appalling. Life without death, they say, would lose all of its meaning and value. It is curious that, whereas some people say that death proves that life is meaningless, others say that it is life without death that would be meaningless, because it is the very knowledge and awareness of our mortality that makes things precious. It is only that which can be lost which can be valued, only that which will not last which can be savoured and treasured.

Pause for a moment now to consider further what you think about death, using the questions in Box 6.2 as a guide.

Box 6.2. Negation or fulfilment?

- Is death the negation of life, making it meaningless? Or is death the fulfilment of life, making it meaningful?
- For you personally, does the prospect of death cast a shadow over life, or shine a light on it?
- To what extent is it the purpose of religion and faith to enable the individual to be reconciled with death?

Responses to bereavement

Whatever we might believe about what death is, or why death is, there is an inescapable truth about death, and it is this: death causes grief. When a person dies, other people grieve. Death challenges us not only intellectually and spiritually, but also emotionally.

Some deaths are less emotionally challenging. The deaths of those whom we don't know personally hardly affect us at all. We can read in the paper about thousands killed in a natural disaster on the other side of the world, and yet remain relatively unmoved. They are people with whom we have no immediate connection, whose lives don't directly touch our hearts. We can read in the paper of the deaths of people in our home country, whose lives are much like ours, and we might be momentarily saddened; but we are not stricken. We know, in our heads, that thousands die each year on our roads, that illness and accidents claim the lives of untold numbers every day, and yet we carry on in our own daily lives unperturbed, believing that the world is a safe place and that life is good.

Then someone whom we love dies, and death is no longer an abstraction. It is something very real. If the deceased has died young, we grieve for their unfulfilled potential, but we grieve mainly for our own loss, the loss of their companionship, the loss of what they meant to us in the daily round, the loss of the ability to love them in real and tangible ways.

The answer that some religions give to the reality of this human grief is to offer the prospect of reunion with the deceased. That reunion might take place at some future time, or it might take place here and now in the form of communication which transcends the barrier between the material and the spiritual worlds. There are some for whom such communication is a primary function of their faith, and some who are very sceptical of it. Where are you on that particular spectrum of beliefs?

Another religious answer to the human grief of bereavement is to seek the spiritual strength to withstand the sadness without recourse to bitterness, to cultivate the spiritual courage to *let go in love.*

Is there a right answer to the reality of our human experience of death, and the grief that it causes us? Use the questions in Box 6.3 to reflect upon a time when you have suffered grief through the death of someone whom you have loved.

Box 6.3. The experience of bereavement, and its impact on faith

- What were the sources of your comfort and strength in that time of sadness?
- Was there a discrepancy between what you believed and what you experienced?
- Did the experience affect your faith, or vice versa?

Unit 7. By whose authority?

In this session we will ask whom we can trust in matters of faith, and how we can know what to believe. In other words, who or what is our ultimate authority in matters of faith and spirituality?

In some religious traditions, ultimate authority resides in a holy book, a scripture in which, it is believed, lie all the answers to all of life's questions, because it has either been written by God or inspired directly by God. The Bible is the ultimate authority for many Christians, as is the Qur'an for Muslims. In some traditions, usually more like cults and sects than legitimate religious faiths, ultimate authority is entrusted to a single individual, and more often than not the cult dies with the person; it can all end very messily. Examples include Jim Jones (1931–1978), the leader of a cult whose members committed mass murders and mass suicides in Jonestown, Guyana, in 1978, and David Koresh (1959–1993) and the fire at the ranch of the Branch Davidians sect in Waco, Texas, in 1993.

In some traditions religious authority lies in a group of individuals or priests who are entrusted with the task of interpretation and prophecy, as well as management of the institution. Those individuals might gain their authority because they have been elected to a position of institutional power, or their power might reside in their knowledge and wisdom, their personal charisma or their political adroitness. In all such cases, the believer decides, 'I will do as I am told. I will follow this leader and I will do what she or he tells me', or 'I will obey the rules of this organisation. I will believe it is true because others wiser than me have said it is true.'

Most religions, in fact, are based on the idea that ultimate authority lies outside the individual. It lies in a book or in a priesthood, or in many years of accumulated tradition and practice, or in a combination of all three. Individual thought and initiative are not only discouraged: they are suppressed, sometimes vigorously. This has been particularly so in those countries in which the church and the state have been interdependent, so that religious heresy has been condemned as sedition or treason against the state and treated just as harshly.

Challenges to external authority

In Europe it was during the sixteenth, seventeenth, and eighteenth centuries that some brave individuals, often at great personal cost, began to challenge the religious orthodoxies of their day. They stood up and said, 'Even though the authorities say this, even though it has been established by the church as the unquestioned truth for centuries, I don't believe it. I think it is wrong, either because it does not conform to the empirical evidence, or because it does not sit squarely with my personal conscience, or I just don't think it makes any sense.' And these brave people have said, 'In matters of faith I will believe what I believe is right, not what you tell me is right'.

The sixteenth-century mathematician and astronomer, Copernicus, argued that Earth was not the centre of the universe. He based his assertion on scientific observation and calculation. But the church insisted that Earth was the centre of the universe. It based its assertion on its faith in scripture, because scripture said that the Earth was the centrepiece of God's creation. The men of the church refused to look through Copernicus' telescope for fear of what they might see, for fear that their own eyes would tell them that they were wrong, and thus that their authority would be undermined. It was more important to them to maintain their authority than to be right in their beliefs. That is a startling illustration, but it is by no means unique. We might scoff at those churchmen from our modern perspective, but none of us likes to have our basic assumptions about the world shaken. We want to trust those in authority.

The power of authority figures

In a great deal of life, we believe something not because we really know anything about it but because we trust the integrity of the person telling us. Public-relations experts know this. They know that if a man in a white lab coat tells us that a washing powder has a special formula to get our shirts clean, we are more inclined to believe him than we are if a woman in a bikini tells us, even if they are both saying exactly the same thing, and even if we know that the man in the lab coat is only an actor, but the woman in the bikini is a real chemist. We don't just believe the words: we believe the person who is speaking the words.

Box 7.1. Whom do you trust?

Think about the people whom you regard as authorities, in whatever sphere: politics, medicine, or religion, for example.
- Can you identify characteristics which they have in common?
- What is likely to make you believe someone?
- Which is more important to you: what is being said, or the identity of the person who is saying it?
- Which people do you instinctively trust, and which do you instinctively distrust?

The power of religious scriptures

For many people, authority resides not so much in a person as in a sacred scripture. Even the physical embodiment of that scripture itself is sacred. Jews handle the Torah with great reverence, and they keep it in a special holy place in the synagogue. Muslims also have a powerful sense of the sacredness of the actual Qur'an. Any violation of the holy book, even dropping it to the floor, is regarded as a terrible insult to Allah. Have there been incidents in your life which revealed your own sense of awe about the Bible or other sacred book? Some people feel uncomfortable about underlining certain passages, or making marginal notes. To them, writing in a holy book can seem disrespectful, even sinful. Others regard such scruples as stupid superstition.

There are many scriptures in the world, but here we are taking the Bible as an example. It is probably the scripture you are most familiar with. What is its authority for you? This is not a trick question. There are no wrong answers. Some people believe that if something is stated in the Bible, then it must be true. Their starting point is that the Bible is the written word of God, so therefore it absolutely cannot be wrong on anything. If passages seem difficult or inconsistent or plain wrong, it must be because of our incomplete understanding.

Other people take a less literalist view. For them the Bible is the principal, even sole, source of religious truth, but it does not trouble them to disregard large sections as irrelevant or unhelpful. As Christians, they regard the Bible as the repository of much wisdom about the nature of God, and the nature of humankind, and the relationship between the two, but they regard the Bible as a human document, written by particular people at particular times in particular contexts. They explore the Bible for whatever value they can glean from it, but they are not unduly uncomfortable if some passages are less helpful than others.

Others again are content to dip into the Bible as it suits them. They value it as a document sacred to others but not to them, and for them something is not necessarily true because it happens to be in the Bible. And still others dismiss the Bible altogether as archaic and irrelevant to their contemporary spiritual exploration. Which of these positions do you lean towards?

Box 7.2. The authority of the Bible and other scriptures

- Do you believe that the Bible is the literal word of God, or is it a book with uniquely great religious value?
- Is it one great book among many books of scripture, or is it irrelevant to your personal spirituality?
- Are there other books, or particular writers, which have made a significant impact on your spiritual life and have become part of your personal scriptures?

Developing individual authority

Let's now look at personal responsibility in developing our spirituality. There is an increasing polarisation in modern spirituality between those who might be called pilgrims and those who are pioneers. On the one hand, there are those who want to hand over to others responsibility for making decisions about what to believe or how to live a spiritual life. They are pilgrims, who concede that others know better than they, and so they entrust the responsibility for their spiritual well-being to those others. They say, in effect, 'Just tell me. I believe you know more than I do, you have experienced more than I have, you have been to the top of the mountain and have seen what is on the other side. Tell me, and I will follow and obey. I will attend your church, I will practise your disciplines, I will pay money to your organisation, because I trust you.'

On the other hand, there are those who insist upon the primacy of their own reason and conscience. Those at this other end of the scale insist upon retaining ultimate responsibility for their own faith choices. They are pioneers. They say, 'You may tell me what you think, and I have a high regard for your learning and experience and I am glad to use them as my guide, but in the end I will decide for myself in matters of my own faith. You may tell me how you live your spirituality, but I will live my own. Let us go to the top of the mountain together.'

One position is not necessarily better than the other. Each has its advantages and strengths. Each has its drawbacks. Whether you are a pilgrim or a pioneer will be determined as much by your psychology as by your theology.

Box 7.3. Are you a pilgrim or a pioneer?

- How do you instinctively respond to a person who claims spiritual authority?
- Some people do seem to have an air of spiritual authority. What are the characteristics of such a person?
- What makes one person a pilgrim and another a pioneer?
- What are the advantages and disadvantages of being a pilgrim?
- What are the advantages and disadvantages of being a pioneer?
- Can you be both a pilgrim and a pioneer?
- Are there more pilgrims or more pioneers in your group?

The need for community

There is much to be said for being in the non-conformist camp. But there are dangers and disadvantages too. One of those dangers is spiritual loneliness. The spiritual path is not always easy, and there are times when we need the company and encouragement of others. It is comforting to know that the path we are following has been successfully followed by others before us, whereas being a pioneer is more experimental. Following a new path might lead to our enlightenment, but it might also get us hopelessly lost and confused.

Another danger is that of spiritual self-delusion. If you think that you are your own ultimate authority, and you test your thoughts and beliefs only in the echo-chamber of your own mind, how can you be sure that you are not just reinforcing your own misconceptions? If you think that everyone is their own ultimate authority, and therefore not likely to yield to anyone else's insights, the logical conclusion is that there is no need for spiritual sharing.

Yet even as pioneers we need not be alone. For most people, meaningful participation in a spiritual community, even one which promotes individual authority, is essential to the health and growth of their personal spirituality. There are very few people with the strength of character to maintain their spiritual health through their own endeavours alone. An essential element of the value of this course is that it can be followed in a community, providing interaction with others, the reassurance that although your paths might diverge from time to time, you are each seeking after the same thing and can help each other in your journeys. To participate in such a spiritual community is not to endow it with ultimate authority to make decisions for you, but it is to use that community as a laboratory of faith in which you test ideas, and – just as important – live out those ideas in meaningful relationship with others.

In recent years there has been an upsurge in the individualisation of spirituality. Many people are inventing their own spiritual path, often using a pick-and-mix approach of taking bits and pieces from various places. But with this growth in individualisation there has often been a loss of appreciation of the role of spiritual community. What do you think is the role of such a community, even for those who are pioneers rather than pilgrims?

Box 7.4. Sources of authority

- How much do you trust your own spiritual authority, and why?
- What is the role of spiritual community in helping you to decide what is true?
- How do you know if something is true?
- What authority, if any, do you ascribe to this course?

Unit 8. Time and history

In this session we ask questions about how the world began. Did it begin according to some grand cosmic design, and is all of history heading towards a pre-determined conclusion? Or did the world begin as a random physical accident, a Big Bang, which had no metaphysical significance and which has no definite end?

In the nineteenth century, Archbishop Ussher of Ireland calculated that the world had been created in the year 4004 BCE. To arrive at this date, he referred only to the Bible, believing as he did that the Bible was the one source of all knowledge about everything in the world. He examined the texts that he thought were relevant, figured out what he believed was the correct chronology of all the events described, and *voilà*: 4004 BCE, the year in which God created the world as reported in the Book of Genesis.

Science and religion: are they mutually exclusive?

Most people today scoff at Ussher's theory. All the scientific evidence points to the absurdity of the Book of Genesis as an historical account of creation. All the disciplines of biology, geology, palaeontology, physics, and astronomy tell us that the world began billions of years ago, probably as the result of a Big Bang. Only people who are wilfully blind to science maintain that Genesis is a true and accurate record of how the world began, and only six thousand years ago at that.

The tragedy is that science and religion so often pit themselves against each other as mutually exclusive. If one is true, the other must be false. The world began as a Big Bang? Therefore the Bible is nonsense. The story of Genesis is true? Therefore science has nothing to say. Whereas the more sophisticated truth is that good science and good religion don't contradict each other – they complement each other by asking different questions. Science addresses the question of how the world began. Religion addresses the very different question of why the world began. Why, and How. Two different questions, and two different ways of answering them. Religion makes itself look ridiculous when it tries to answer scientific questions. And science makes itself ridiculous when it tries to answer religious questions or, what is more often the case, when it tries to dismiss the validity of religious questions.

So, how old is the universe? How did it begin? Scientists continue to argue over the details of their theories. That's what scientists are supposed to do – dispute with each other over what the empirical evidence is telling them. Scientists look at the evidence, in a laboratory, under the microscope and at the end of a telescope, and they try to fit the pieces together into an explanation which makes sense. The answers to their questions will not be found in the scriptures of any religion, whether Judaeo-Christian or any other.

Does that make the Genesis story of creation untrue? Or, more accurately, the Genesis stories, because in fact there are two stories of creation in Genesis, and they can't both be right, because they are each quite different. As science and as history, the stories in Genesis have no factual validity. The world did not come about as Genesis tells us. However, that does not mean that those stories are untrue. The book of Genesis is a myth. A myth is not a piece of make-believe, and it is not something that is false. A myth is a story which expresses a basic belief about the world and our place in it. A myth is true if it helps us to understand in ways other than the factual.

Are you familiar with the plays of William Shakespeare? There was never any such person as Othello. He is a product of Shakespeare's dramatic imagination. But, to dismiss Othello as untrue because his tragic story did not really happen is to entirely miss the point of the play, which is an exploration of the destructive power of jealousy, an emotion which is part of the human condition. The play's abiding truth is that, regardless of whether or not a man called Othello ever actually killed his wife

Desdemona, we recognise something of ourselves in him, and perhaps also in Iago, the villain of the play.

Likewise, the point of the creation stories of Genesis is to explore the human experience of living in a world created not by us but by powers or forces beyond our comprehension, and through which we not only touch the material world but receive hints of a divine presence. People look at the world and they see power and mystery and magnificence. Some people see intelligence and order and majesty. They look at the world, and through what they see and the response that it evokes they experience the presence of God. They say: the world is divine, the world is holy, because God is in the world. That experience of the presence of God through the wonder of the world is true and profound, regardless of how the world actually came into being.

For some, that God of creation is a personal God, who willed the world into being at some specific point in time, perhaps much as the story of Genesis narrates. And for some, God is more of a metaphorical way of understanding that which transcends the finite and the time-bound. In other words, to say that God created the world is, for some, a statement of literal historical fact, but for others it is a poetic way of expressing a profound spiritual truth. For that latter group, the world is the medium through and beyond which they see something of the nature of God. It means that the world is holy, sacred, worthy of our highest respect and reverence, not to be regarded merely as the object of intellectual curiosity, and certainly not to be desecrated by the mean and the lowly.

Box 8.1 contains questions designed to help you to shape and share your thoughts about creation.

Box 8.1. What does the creation myth mean to you?

- What do you believe is the relationship between God and the creation of the world?
- What can be learned from creation stories such as those found in the Book of Genesis?
- Are you familiar with other religious myths about how the world began?
- Are science and religion complementary or adversarial?
- Which are more important to you – the 'how' questions of science or the 'why' questions of religion?

The quest for purpose, meaning, and value

The purpose of religion is not to answer the question of *how* the world was created, but *why* it was created. In other words, religion tells a story about the world so that it sets the context for meaningful human living.

That is where science is found wanting. Science provides no emotional context. It might be the case that the world just happened. There was a massive explosion, a spontaneous combustion of energy from which was flung the ever-expanding universe that we know today. That might explain the science, but it leaves the heart and the spirit hungry and unsatisfied. The scientific explanation is emotionally and spiritually barren. It provides no moral context. It leaves everything to accident and chance, and it offers no compelling story about the universe within which we can find meaning, purpose, and value for our own lives.

Yet your experience of life may tell you that it is more purposeful and profound than mere chance. In our own lives we want to discover purpose, meaning, and value. Can there be meaning in our own small life in a universe which is pure randomness? It seems difficult. Our individual lives must be pointless if the world is pointless. So there is a spiritual desire for the universe to have purpose, meaning, and value within which our own life can have purpose, meaning, and value too.

Religion addresses this biggest of questions. Why did the world begin, and what is its ultimate destination? As there was a beginning, what will be the end? And the meta-narrative about that end-point for all of creation sets the context within which we might discover our own personal end-point and purpose.

There are different points of view on this. For some, their spiritual destination within the larger context of the history of the world is very personal. It is about the perfection of their own soul. The world itself will continue as a material entity, but within that, yet removed from it, is the individual's task to grow his or her own soul to completeness. For others, the spiritual destination entails the very destruction of the world. They believe that their spiritual destiny will be completed only with the annihilation of the world and all that they regard as the world's wickedness. Such apocalyptic visions form the centrepiece of some manifestations of Christianity and other faiths, where the spiritual life is one of constant preparedness for the end-time – in spite of repeated disappointments.

Even if you dismiss as folly the prospect of a divinely orchestrated end to the world's wickedness by the violent imposition of a new order, as prophesied by some, it is a real possibility that the world, or at least our human inhabitation of it, will be ended by our own hand. We have built nuclear arsenals capable of destroying the world many times over, and although the risk of their use has diminished in the past decade or so, their possession and threatened deployment remain central to the so-called defence policies of many national governments. Humankind, and all other life, might yet be destroyed in an instant through the vainglory or incompetence of a handful of politicians. Less spectacular but no less likely is the prospect of the death of the planet through gradual environmental destruction. We could slowly suffocate and starve ourselves through our obstinate collective refusal to change our way of being on the planet. Is this just a new interpretation of an old myth – that God will destroy the world and is simply using us humans as his agents on Earth to bring it about? Would it matter if life on Earth did end?

Some take a more phlegmatic view. If this is just one tiny planet in one small galaxy, and there are thousands of galaxies with millions of planets, if it was only an accident that life should have started here in the first place, would it matter if it were to end? It might matter to us, in an immediate and selfish kind of way, but would it matter on the cosmic scale? Would it matter to God? Although we have accepted that Earth is not the centre of everything, as the ancients believed, it is the centre of our everything. Earth is where we live. It is our home. If it is to be destroyed, by whatever cause, will it matter? Box 8.2 poses some of these big questions.

Box 8.2. The end of the world

- What do you think is the future of Earth?
- How does that ultimate future affect how you live now?
- Does it make you fatalistic or hopeful?
- Is your personal spiritual salvation separate from the future of the planet, or intensely dependent upon it?

We turn now to consider whether we are active agents in the making of our own history.

Masters of the universe?

To what extent do you believe that we humans are, or should be, active agents? Do you believe that we are God's representatives on Earth, specifically charged to exercise dominion over the rest of creation, and that it is part of our spiritual responsibility to be worthy custodians of the planet? Or is it our spiritual responsibility to relinquish the arrogance of assuming that we ever had that privileged role, and our proper spiritual task is to be in tune with the rest of creation, not to intervene as masters but to assimilate as co-participants?

Whether you believe that it was chance or divine intention that we humans evolved in the way that we have, the fact is that we do have the power of speech and thought, we do engage with abstract ideas and create beauty of word, vision, and song. We have evolved into a privileged and powerful position in creation, but does that mean that we are special in the eyes of God? In Victorian times, after Darwin's theories had revolutionised the way in which people thought about the natural world, a commonly held belief was that humanity was in a continuing state of evolution and would gradually grow from its affinity with the animal world into a close affinity with the divine. In other words, the end-point of evolution would be human social perfection. Paradise would be regained not through an apocalyptic external event, but through our own labours. That late-Victorian optimism, born of a time of great social improvement and scientific change, suffered a cruel disillusionment through the horrors of the twentieth century, but some people still cling to that belief. Others believe that we are condemned never to learn from history but to repeat the same mistakes, again and again and again.

The universe is billions of years old. Science tells us that if we were to condense that history into a 24-hour time period, what we know as the whole of human history, namely the last ten thousand years or so, would be but the last second or two before midnight. The time-scale of an individual human life is so ephemeral as to be of virtually no consequence. And yet our own life is all we have. We are each a part of the story of the universe. That is part of the human dilemma: to be aware on the one hand of how insignificant we each are, and yet on the other hand to believe ourselves to have infinite value. How do we reconcile those two extremes?

Now some questions for you to consider in your group as the conclusion to this session.

Box 8.3. Ourselves in the context of eternity

- To what extent is your personal story determined by the story of the world?
- If your personal safety could be guaranteed, what epoch in the history of the world would you like to visit, and why?
- Describe your own vision of heaven on earth.

Unit 9. The importance of belief

In this session we will look at the role of belief. How important is what we actually believe?

Many people assume that to be religious is to hold particular prescribed beliefs. Conversely, they suppose that if you don't hold those beliefs, you are therefore not religious. However, one of the assumptions underpinning the *Life Spirit* course is that you don't have to subscribe to a set of fixed beliefs in order to be religious, or in order to be spiritually active. The assumption is that being spiritually active, even being religiously active, is more about how you live than about what you say you believe.

This unit explores the role and importance of beliefs. Beliefs are certainly important. But we will also explore the difference between beliefs *that* some things are a certain way, which might or might not be true, and belief *in* something. Belief in something is an issue of faith. It is not just an intellectual idea. It is something to which you commit yourself. Believing *in* something demands that you commit yourself to it with your mind – but more importantly with your heart, your soul, and your daily actions.

As was explored in more detail in Unit 3 on personal faith, organised religion, and particularly Christianity, has often been side-tracked into detailed argument about beliefs that are intellectual propositions. The theologians of the early Christian church, for example, argued endlessly about Jesus and the nature of his relationship with God. In fact, they were so busy arguing about Jesus that they neglected to follow his teachings.

The most important development in this process of refining beliefs happened in the year 325, as we have noted before, when Emperor Constantine convened a council of bishops at Nicaea to devise a creed.

The Nicene Creed (slightly revised in 381) has remained essentially unchanged ever since, and is recited Sunday after Sunday by the Christian faithful. It starts with the words, 'I believe' and goes on to make a number of statements about who Jesus was and what happened to him after he had been crucified, and what it all meant. Some of you might recite that creed every Sunday when you go to church. Others of you might not even have heard of it. Whether or not the statements in that creed are true is not for us to decide here. But they are 'belief *that*' statements. They don't necessarily have any impact on how you live.

Beliefs are undoubtedly important. There are good beliefs and there are bad beliefs. There are beliefs which are well founded on experience, and there are beliefs which aren't. There are beliefs which affect our behaviour, and there are beliefs which are irrelevant to the way we live. For your group conversation now, try to answer the 'belief *that*' statements in Box 9.1 with a simple Yes or No. More interestingly, having answered them and shared your own answers with the group, then discuss why you believe them, or not, and what impact they do or do not have on your spiritual life.

Box 9.1. Believing *that* ...

Do you answer Yes or No to the following assertions?
- God created the world.
- Jesus was crucified by the Roman authorities.
- My death will be the end of all of my personal consciousness.
- The Bible is the infallible Word of God.
- God will bring the world to an apocalyptic end and establish his kingdom of the righteous for all time.

Let's now look more closely at the differences between beliefs *that*, and belief *in*. To illustrate the difference, consider what you believe about the Sun.

You might say that you believe that the Sun will rise in the east tomorrow morning. If asked why you believe that, you might reply that every morning of your life so far that is what has happened, and although the past cannot guarantee the future, you will go to bed this evening in the expectation that the Sun will do what it has always done in the past. You might also predict the exact time when the Sun would rise, based on detailed observation and calculation. It would not be possible to survive in the world without those kinds of basic assumption and belief. In the morning, you would be shown to have been right.

What, however, if you said you believed that the Sun rotates around the Earth, as used to be the established belief? You might be asked the reason for such a belief. If you tried to justify your belief on empirical grounds, you would probably be dismissed as a crank or a fool, because you were in defiance of all the scientific community.

What if you said that you believed that the Sun rotates around the Earth because that is what was believed approximately two thousand years ago when the religious teacher whom you follow was alive, and the book that records all of that religious teacher's sayings shows unambiguously that he said that the Sun orbits the Earth? You are a faithful follower of this teacher, whose spiritual wisdom you trust and who seems to speak many truths about life, so you therefore believe that he must also be right about the Sun. Again, the secular scientific world might laugh you to scorn. But is it a reasonable defence for you to say that you believe the Sun rotates around the Earth because someone whom you trust and follow in other ways has said so? We are back to the issue of religious authority, as explored in Unit 7.

However, what if you did not say that you believed the Sun orbits the Earth – something which is open to empirical study, able to be proved or disproved – but you said you believed that the Sun was God? As far as the science is concerned, you might gladly concede what others more qualified tell you: that it is a massive ball of energy, exuding light and heat, around which the planets of our solar system circle. But your belief that the Sun is God would be unaffected by such scientific observations, because your religious belief is not open to empirical scrutiny. It cannot be proved or disproved in the same way. What might be manifestly true, however, is that you are a faithful, kind, and decent person, and you claim that you are who you are because of your belief that the Sun is God.

This might seem fanciful, but consider what some people say about God. They say they believe in God as energy, light, love, kindness, creative force. No one doubts that these qualities are real. The question of belief is whether they are manifestations of God, or just knowable phenomena.

We need to make a very important distinction here. The distinction is between believing *that* certain statements are true, and believing *in* something. So, you believe *that* the Sun is the centre of our solar system, around which Earth and the other planets orbit. You believe *that* it is the source of light and energy which is the very life-force for us on Earth, without which no life would be possible. You believe *that* at some time in the very distant future the Sun will eventually exhaust itself of heat and light. In those beliefs, you are no different from scientists who study the Sun, who explain the physics of what it is and how it functions and how we benefit from it.

Your belief *in* the Sun as God is something quite different, because that suggests not only an intellectual agreement with various statements about physical, scientific facts: it suggests that you have committed yourself to living in a certain way, that your belief is as much a matter of the heart as of the mind, and that it requires of you certain emotional and spiritual responses.

Many of the things that we believe to be the case are irrelevant to how we live. You may believe that it gets very cold in the Antarctic. You believe it because people who have been there have all said the same thing. Unless you intend visiting the far north, and will need to remember to pack your long underwear, that belief does not affect your daily life. Many beliefs are irrelevant to our religious life, even if they might ostensibly be in the field of religion. For example, the belief that Jesus did in fact live and that he was crucified by the Roman authorities. Some people question whether or not he was a real person – some people say he is the product of imaginative myth-making. But believing that Jesus did live and was crucified does not necessarily say anything about how you will live your life, or that Jesus will necessarily be central to your spirituality. Many people are happy to concede that Jesus was a real person, but they have no interest in his teachings or the possibility of his life having a continuing impact on theirs. They believe things about him, but they do not believe *in* him.

Faith and spirituality are a matter of belief *in*, much more than belief *that*. Spirituality is about the heart and what you commit yourself to, what fashions your life, and how you want to be in the world. What is important is not the belief itself, but the type of person you are because of that belief: how that belief shapes and sustains you, and what you do to nurture and develop that belief.

Is it not the case that two people can share the same belief and yet be very different kinds of people? Let's say, two people sit side by side in a church and together they recite the Nicene Creed. Both of them sincerely believe every word of what they recite. And one of them is a kind, gentle, loving person of manifest spiritual authenticity, and the other is a cruel, violent, and unpleasant individual whose spirituality is a sham. Their intellectual beliefs are identical, yet the quality of their lives is so different.

Is it not also the case that two people can hold diametrically opposite beliefs and yet be the same kind of person? Let us suppose that one is a Christian and the other a Hindu. They are alike in the goodness of their character, their delight in the world, the gifts of love that they generously bestow on those around them, because although their beliefs about things might differ, their belief *in* essential values, the things they commit their hearts and their lives to, are the same.

Box 9.2 contains some seemingly simple questions for you to consider and discuss.

Box 9.2. Believing *in* ...

- What do you believe *in*? Can you identify just one thing that you believe in which governs your life and to which you commit yourself?
- What does that belief mean in terms of how you live?
- What are the beliefs *that* which follow from your belief *in*?
- How important is it that what you believe in is based on what is objectively true?

Here is another way to think about the difference between beliefs *that*, and believing *in*. Consider someone who lives in a brick terrace house. The house has the usual complement of rooms – living room, dining room, kitchen, bedrooms, bathrooms, and so on. It is a terrace house not unlike millions of other terrace houses in the United Kingdom. It is made of bricks and wood and glass and steel. Some of the mid-nineteenth-century period features add charm to the house, but the person who lives there does not really care about them. The physical details of the house are not in the least bit important. He has no emotional attachment whatever to the individual bricks which make up the house. But he has a strong emotional attachment to his home. His home is not just the house in which he lives: it is the place where his heart lies, which he shares with others whom he loves, where he plays out his life with all of its joys and disappointments and hurts. He loves his home. He feels safe in his home, even though he knows that statistically it is one of the most dangerous places to be. More accidents happen in the home than anywhere else. And his home is the most dangerous place for him not only in a physical sense: he knows that in his home he risks some of the worst heart wounds possible. But it is where he wants to be. It is where he chooses to be.

Beliefs are the building blocks in the house of one's personal faith. The individual beliefs are not important, other than that they are sound and strong and able to fulfil their function. What is important is the house of personal faith created with those building blocks of belief. You don't form emotional attachments to individual bricks or individual stones or pieces of timber in your house. You form emotional attachments to your home of faith and everything that house means to you, and in doing so you make it your spiritual home.

Of course it is not only what the house is made of which makes it your home. It is what you do in it: the daily, weekly rituals that you might never have thought about as being rituals, but the regular repetition of which become an integral part of your being in that space. Think about a typical day in your home. You wake up. Do you lie in bed for a while, or do you immediately start your day? You make your first cup of tea or coffee. Do you have a favourite cup? Do you like to do it in a particular way? Then breakfast. Sitting down at a properly set table, or on the hoof as you get yourself dressed and ready for the day for which you are already running late? Do you have a ritual for when you return home? Do you put your keys in the same place, do you take off your shoes, make yourself a drink, sit in 'your' chair?

And the weekly rituals? The cleaning of the house, the doing of chores? Do you have particular days when you do the laundry, the dusting, the vacuuming? Do you do the chores in a special order? All of this becomes a habitual and ritualised way in which you establish being in your home. You might believe many things about your home: that you own it, that it is worth so much money should you want to sell it, or that you pay a fair – or excessive – rent for it, that it is in a good neighbourhood, that the roof needs mending. But you believe in your home as a place where you belong, which you have made your own.

Box 9.3 offers some final questions to ponder.

Box 9.3. The bricks of belief in the home of faith

- Is being a person of faith about holding the right beliefs?
- Is being a person of faith about believing in something to which you commit yourself?
- Are beliefs intellectual propositions, or emotional attachments?
- Write down and share with your group five statements beginning with the words 'I believe *that*...'. And one statement which begins with the words 'I believe *in*...'. How is your belief *in* statement related to your belief *that* statements?

Unit 10. God

In this session we come to one of the biggest and most profound of all religious questions. It is the question from which all other spiritual questions follow. Does God exist? And if so, what kind of God?

A lot of people seem to think that the existence of God is a simple yes/no question. Do you believe in God, they ask, yes or no? If only it were that simple! The question of God is extremely complex, and it is very easy to get caught up in digressions which lead nowhere useful or productive.

Ways of shaping the divine

Let's start with a very brief history of God. For the sake of simplicity, we shall here use the singular word, God, but we shall take it to include multiple gods and goddesses. Virtually all cultures and civilisations throughout history have had some concept of God which has been central not only to their understanding of how the world came to be and was organised, but also how we as people should live in harmony with the world and with each other. God has been a central figure in the ordering of human affairs, public and private morality, and understandings of the meaning of life and our ultimate destiny beyond death. For most of that history, in most manifestations, God has been portrayed in human form – only with infinitely more power, wisdom, and authority than we have. God, in other words, has been real.

There is a good reason for this, and the reason is that in speaking of God we are speaking of what is beyond our immediate human knowledge, but the only tools we have at our disposal are those within human knowledge. We use what we do know in order to talk about what we do not know. And so people have used metaphors for God from the human world – monarch, judge, warrior, creator, inventor, father, friend – to describe that God, and we have projected our human emotions on to God. So, for example, in Jewish, Greek, Roman, and Egyptian mythologies, God feels jealousy and love, anger and forgiveness, pettiness and generosity. God has been made super-human.

Such an understanding of God used to fit well when our scientific comprehension of the natural world was limited. God was also the author of natural phenomena – earthquakes and floods, thunder and lightning. Natural phenomena were interpreted as signs of God's pleasure or disapproval. They were the consequences, perhaps, of our human activity, and God could be persuaded, through prayer or ritual sacrifice or the promise of future good behaviour, to bring rains to end drought, or sunshine to end flood.

As scientific knowledge has expanded, and our understanding of the natural world has seemingly displaced God as the direct agent of weather, there has arisen in the minds of some a stark conflict between the claims of science and the claims of religion. Some people have abandoned all notion of God, because they cannot reconcile such an undeveloped God with what they now know is scientifically true. Others refuse to acknowledge the discoveries of science, because to do so would compromise their steadfast clinging to their ancient God.

What do you know about the perception of God as a real agent of history and the world? Whether or not you believe now in such a God, or in the gods or goddesses of other mythologies, what do you know about how different cultures, religions, and mythologies have interpreted the role of God? Are you familiar with Greek and Roman mythologies? Have you read classics such as *The Odyssey*, which portray the gods as living somewhere other, on Mount Olympus or in the heavens, but who meddle in human affairs as the whim takes them, who have their own society and hierarchy and responsibilities?

Box 10.1 offers some questions to prompt your discussion. Remember, this is about what you know about what has been believed in the past about God or gods or goddesses, not about what you might believe now.

Box 10.1. A brief history of God

- What roles has God been given? For example, king, shepherd, judge? Can you cite further examples?
- What human emotions have been attributed to God?
- In what ways has God been perceived as interfering with or controlling human destiny?
- How did such a God create the world?

How was your discussion about God, or gods, as an active agent in history – human, only infinitely more so? Perhaps you started to see how helpful it has been, in many ways, to use human language and imagery to speak about that which is beyond the human, but also how it can lead us into difficulty and absurdity. Much of the difficulty and absurdity that plagues our God-talk arises when we talk as if we are speaking definitively.

Images of God

It is important to remember that when we speak of God, we are using the language of poetry and metaphor. Poetry expresses things in ways which perhaps are not immediately obvious, but the beauty and truth of which expand, challenge, and enrich our appreciation of our human experience. So, when Robert Burns exclaims 'My love is like a red, red rose', we don't interpret that literally. We don't think, oh, Burns's girlfriend has petals and thorns and grows in the dirt and will die at the end of summer. We know that he is expressing something about his appreciation of her beauty, and how he responds to that beauty.

God as Judge

Likewise, people have said something like, 'God is my judge'. What might that mean? If you take it literally, how would it work? Consider the role of a magistrate. She is accustomed to sitting in court, listening to the evidence and declaring that people are guilty or not guilty, and passing sentence accordingly. Should we see God as the supreme magistrate? Does saying that 'God is my judge' mean that, either at regular intervals or finally at the end of your life, you will be brought into God's celestial court and the catalogue of your crimes and misdemeanours will be read out, perhaps the list of your good deeds also, and you will be deemed either worthy or unworthy, and sentenced accordingly? Sent off to an eternity of punishment, or to an eternity of reward? That is what some people believe, and certainly the idea of ultimate judgement is a belief which has dominated mainstream Christian thought. But if you take it literally, it is not long before you enter into the realms of absurdity. When you start to ask, 'OK, but exactly how will that celestial court function, and will I have a counsel for my defence, and do I get legal aid?', then such a belief does start to stretch one's credulity.

But if you understand the phrase 'God is my judge' poetically, it can mean something very different: it can mean that there is a sense in which you feel you are ultimately accountable for your actions, a sense in which you cannot plead innocence when you know you are guilty, a place in which there is no hiding from the essence of who you are. God can be a poetic expression of that ultimate accountability. God is the still, small voice of conscience which only the psychopath lacks.

When you use poetic language about God, you are not describing God; you are describing your experience of God, and that is a very different thing.

It is very tempting to slip from the poetic to the literal. Our minds find it easier to think in concrete terms. But in speaking of God, it is a temptation to be resisted, lest too soon we fall into the dangers of destroying the very thing that we are trying to describe. It is curious how, when speaking about God, many people preface their remarks by saying that God is beyond their understanding, and then immediately describe God in great detail, and with absolute insistence on the correctness of their description, and zero tolerance for anybody's else's description. The history of talking about God is littered with examples of this intolerance. Here is a word of friendly advice: be very wary of anyone who tells you with great authority that they know what God is like, or what God wants. They don't. Nobody does.

Now that you have been warned of the dangers of doing so, let's talk about God. What are some of the other poetic metaphors that have been used about God, and what might they mean? What are we saying about the qualities that we identify as godlike when we use various metaphors? Remember: we are not describing God, we are speaking about our experience of God.

God as Father and/or Mother

What about God as Father, one of the most common and popular metaphors? Even this is fraught with problems, because some people struggle with the role of being a father, or their relationship with their father is a source of pain. The metaphor speaks of an idealised image of fatherhood. That image portrays the father as a loving figure of gentle but firm authority, protective, wanting what is best for his children. God the father has a larger and wiser view of the world than the child, and can offer good counsel and emotional support and guidance. We seek the approval of such a father figure, and flourish in his favour.

Originally scandalous and heretical, but more and more accepted, is the image of God as Mother. it is logistically absurd, of course, to be both father and mother, but remember, this is poetry, in which two things can both be true even if they are contradictory in reality. The motherhood of God speaks of God as the nurturer, the giver and sustainer of life, to whose bosom we return for comfort and warmth.

God as King

The image of God as King has been much used. Human societies are organised in various ways, but most have some sense of class or caste, based perhaps on the accident of birth or on what is achieved in life through education or occupation. Particularly in those societies with a firmly entrenched social hierarchy, each class is placed within a context of subordination. The serf is subordinate to the lord, the lord is subordinate to the king, who is master of all. So God is perceived as King of all, the ultimate power to whom even worldly monarchs must owe obedience.

God as Watchmaker

And finally, God as Watchmaker. There is a view (expressed in various different forms) that the world is like a fantastically intricate watch which God designed, made, wound up, and set going. And then God perhaps lost interest in our world and went off and left us to it. The eighteenth-century British theologian William Paley (1743–1805) most famously put forward this idea. Supposing you were out walking, he said, and you discovered a watch in the middle of a heath. You would conclude from the fact of the intricacy of the watch that there had been a watchmaker. Similarly, the world is intricate and wonderful, so there must have been someone who made it. In other words: God.

The dangers of literalism

All of these metaphors, and others, taken literally, can quickly lead to absurdity and be easily repudiated. Some modern writers have made their names by demolishing belief in a literal God. Belief in a literal God is very difficult to reconcile with the modern world of science and philosophy. But such writers are as literalistic in their unbelief in God as others are in their belief. All that can ever be said about God has to be said in metaphor and poetry, and when we use such metaphors we are not describing God, we are speaking about our experience of the divine, about that which lifts us up beyond the mundane to the world of wonder, mystery, and reverence.

If particular metaphors don't work for you, if they fail to lift you up into a spirit of reverence, then here is what to do. Acknowledge graciously that other people find those metaphors helpful, and continue to seek the metaphors that you will find helpful. Just as different kinds of poetry appeal to different people, so different metaphors for God will speak differently according to how they resonate with personal, subjective experience.

Which metaphors about God do work for you? Discuss with your group which metaphors you like or do not like, identifying if you can why they do or do not speak to you. Box 10.2 contains some metaphors that you might like to consider.

Box 10.2. Metaphors for God

Do any of the following metaphors resonate with your own experience?

- God as Judge
- God as Father
- God as Mother
- God as King
- God as Warrior
- God as Shepherd
- God as Law Giver
- God as Teacher

Can you think of other metaphors for God?

God is not a thing

So far, the metaphors that we have been discussing have been things that exist in our real world. We know what a father is, what a king is, what a shepherd is. Those things exist. We can point to them and say, 'That thing is a father'.

Things are bound by time and space. However, if we ask the question, 'Does God exist?', what are we asking? Are we suggesting that God exists in the same way as other things exist, that God can be pointed to as a separate thing, and we can say without ambiguity 'That is God'? No. Even believers in God do not think of God in that way. We have been talking about the need for subtlety of language and elasticity of thought in using metaphors about God. Equally, we need to be subtle and elastic in our use of the word 'exist' when discussing God. We can't speak of God as existing in the same way as we talk about trees and people and animals existing, because to do so is to reduce God to being just one more separate thing among a multitude of other things. God is not a thing.

However, there are realities which do exist but not in the way that things exist. These are the spiritual realities. No one can deny that love, and hope, and goodness, and compassion exist, but they do not exist as things. They are qualities, experiences, emotions, aspirations. So if we talk of God existing, we have to do so with the understanding that we are using the concept of 'existing' in the same sense that we use when speaking of spiritual realities. Spiritual realities are not bound by time and space. They transcend them.

How do you connect with this spiritual reality of God? That is the question which underpins all religions, all spiritual practices, all aspirations of the individual human heart for that which is eternal and universal. Religions in their various ways have developed different techniques and practices for connecting with spiritual reality. Some have done it through learning and study, some through meditation and prayer, some through fasting and physical activity, or through communing with the world of nature.

In Unit 2, on Spirituality, we consider the feeling of being connected. For example, feeling connected with the universe when you look up into the star-lit heavens. You might not believe that God created the world as reported in the Book of Genesis, preferring instead to believe what scientists tell you: that the universe came into being several billion years ago as the result of a massive explosion of energy and matter – a Big Bang. But we can still talk about creation being divine. However this universe began, and for whatever reason, there is life on this small out-of-the way planet called Earth. There is experience of life that is not just random and meaningless. There is meaning, because you seek it and, sometimes, you may feel fleetingly as if you have found it. There is no single, exclusive Meaning of Life. But we give meaning to life as we live it and as we reflect on it. We can be content to use the word 'God' as a way of describing the process by which our spirits rise up out of the ordinary and the mundane to aspire to something nobler and more sacred. God is that which gives meaning to life beyond mere existence. God is the context for the connections that make life divine.

Another view of God is immanence. God is not out there in the universe, but is the divinity within every one of us. That divinity manifests itself as the quiet, persistent voice of conscience, the call to duty, to do what is right, not what is expedient. It is the immanent God which reaches out in love and mercy to others, and which responds to the promptings of beauty. A spirituality which is grounded in that concept of God seeks to harmonise the outer world of human activity with the inner world of personal divinity. This understanding of God is often more likely to be found in the writings and experiences of mystics who look inwards rather than outwards for their revelations. This God acts in the world not as an interventionist cosmic agent, but through the works of spiritually enlightened individuals. This God is a spirit, a benign influence, that which elevates and inspires. This God is not 'real' in the sense of being in a particular time or space. When speaking of this God, you do not say, 'This is God', but rather, 'I feel the presence of God'. God does not move towards you in the hope that you will respond; you move in the midst of God until you come into harmony and focus.

You have an opportunity now to discuss this concept of God as spirit, not as something objectively real. Box 10.3 contains some questions that you might like to consider.

Box 10.3. Does God exist?

- Can you have a relationship with something that does not exist?
- If so, what kind of relationship might that be, and how could you cultivate it?
- Does God respond?
- How do you know God?

Religion without God?

Is it possible to have a spirituality without any concept of God at all, as either a transcendent being or as an immanent presence? What would such a spirituality look like?

Buddhism is not focused on a deity. It is not dependent on belief in the existence of a God or gods, yet it has a highly developed spirituality, based on a deeply humanistic understanding of life. The practice of Buddhism is the practice of inwardness and mindfulness, the practice of living as if each and every moment is holy, and the aim of life is to discover and experience that holiness. You could argue that this is similar to a concept of God as immanence, and certainly there are similarities. But Buddhism specifically rejects the idea of deity.

Many Western humanists who have no use for a deity and are not Buddhists seek to cultivate their spirituality solely through the realm of human experience. In the human arts they find their beauty. In the world of nature they find their solace. In the world of personal encounter they find their meaning.

In Unit 9 we discussed the role and importance of belief, and made the distinction between believing things *about* something and believing *in* something. Beliefs *about* are intellectual ideas which may be true or false, but which do not necessarily mean anything about who we are or what is important to us. But to believe *in* something is to orientate your life towards it. You might have many beliefs *about* God, none of which means anything. But believing *in* God, whether or not you have a belief that there is such a thing as God, means committing yourself to spiritual realities: it means living in such a way that you make God real in your life.

In that sense, do you believe *in* God? Do you make God real in your life?

Box 10.4. God in daily life

• Think about the beliefs that you have previously shared *about* God, and consider their impact on your daily practice of spirituality.
• In other words, how do you translate your beliefs *about* God into believing *in* God?

Unit 11. Suffering and evil

In this session we will ask some of the most troubling questions about life: why is there suffering, and how can we respond to it so that we are not spiritually destroyed by it?

In classic theology there is a dilemma known as the Problem of Evil. Simply stated, it goes like this. There are two things which are believed to be true about God. God is all-powerful. And God is all-good. However, it is empirically true that there is evil in the world. That must mean either that God chooses not to do anything about it, in which case God is not all-good. Or God is unable to do anything about it, in which case God is not all-powerful. It cannot be the case that all three propositions are true: God is All-Good, God is All-Powerful, and there is evil in the world. Only two can be true. Which one do you discard?

One answer put forward by those who refuse to compromise the twin attributes of God as all-good and all-powerful has been to deny the reality of suffering and evil. The latter might seem like suffering and evil to us, but that is only because of our inferior and inadequate understanding of the situation. In fact, everything is all part of the plan for the greater good, which will be made known in the fullness of time, and our duty meanwhile is to accept whatever happens as part of the grand plan.

Another answer is that suffering is the necessary crucible through which we are spiritually purified and grow as individuals. It is observably true that some people do face and overcome significant suffering in their lives and emerge from their ordeal much more strong, resilient, and faithful. However, is it justified to force someone else to suffer because you believe that their suffering might be a God-given opportunity for their spiritual growth? Is it justified to insist on another's suffering for the sake of your own spiritual growth? Can we say that suffering is the necessary price that we should be willing to pay for our spiritual enlightenment? Because it is also observably true that some suffering leads to no such enlightenment. Some people are left not spiritually enlarged but demonstrably diminished by their suffering. They become embittered, shrivelled of soul. Or they simply endure, and then die. The question remains: does even the possibility of spiritual enlightenment justify suffering?

A conundrum is that some of the principal sources of our pain and anguish are also the sources of our greatest delight. Our joy and our sorrow are inextricably linked. In seeking joy, we risk sorrow. In enduring sorrow, we can discover joy. To enter into a loving relationship with another is to know that the other person will at times almost certainly cause you pain, and that you will cause them pain. It cannot be avoided. Yet not to enter into a loving relationship because you are afraid of that pain is to remain emotionally stunted and unfulfilled.

Box 11.1 poses some difficult questions.

Box 11.1. Suffering as a condition of life

- How do you explain suffering?
- Do you think that God is not all-good and all-powerful – or do you think that suffering is not real?
- Can you think of instances in which you have experienced suffering in the realm of human relationships, either as its cause or as its victim?
- How has your own suffering affected you spiritually, for better or for worse?

We need to say something important here about the difference between sitting back and pontificating as an observer of suffering and actually being in the thick of it. Our intellectual attitude towards suffering while we are well fed, in good health, and free from pain is likely to be very different from what it would be like if we were to be stricken by a crippling, painful illness. There is a temptation to be glib about suffering as an abstraction when we are not directly experiencing it. However, thinking about the meaning of suffering while not experiencing it directly can help us to understand and prepare for suffering when it does visit us.

Different kinds of suffering

Not all suffering arises from human relationships, of course. There are different kinds of suffering. There is the suffering caused through illness, accident, and death. As we explored in Unit 6, death is the inescapable price that we pay for being alive. But some people do not meet death until the fullness of their life is over, and some meet death early and unfairly. Some slip gently into that good night, and some endure great physical pain or emotional distress before they finally depart this life. Life is a fickle mistress. Part of suffering is the feeling of not deserving it, of feeling unfairly treated. *Why me?*

There is also the suffering caused by natural events and misfortunes. Think about a great natural disaster – an earthquake, for example, which kills many people. The suffering of the people directly affected by that disaster is very real. There are the deaths of those killed, the injuries of many others, and the grief of those who have lost loved ones or who have been made homeless and destitute; their suffering is not only in the immediate moment, but protracted over a long period of time. All of that suffering is real. But is suffering caused by natural events spiritually different from suffering caused by deliberate human malice or carelessness?

In whatever guise it might appear, through human encounter or the natural world, suffering often makes people turn to their spirituality, either seeking solace or questioning their previously held belief that somehow faith would protect them against such misfortune. However, the cause of the suffering itself is frequently morally neutral. It is simply an event which happens, and to which we must respond.

Or is it? Some suffering we certainly bring upon ourselves through our own actions. We continue to smoke, even though we know it is very likely to cause us to die miserably of lung cancer. We eat badly and to excess, even though we know that a poor diet, or obesity, can lead to a multitude of health problems. We know there are some identifiable causes which lead to identifiable effects.

Coming to terms with suffering

Is this true of all suffering? There are many faiths and theologies which say that we invite cosmic suffering and misfortune through our own actions. We have bad karma. Our spiritual ill-health leaves us vulnerable to physical disease. Our broken relationship with God exposes us to danger and despair. Or, our suffering is a direct punishment by God for our misdeeds. There are many stories told in the great religions of peoples or individuals being visited with great suffering because of their transgressions. People often ask, *'Why me? What did I do to deserve this great sadness? Did I do something wrong? Is this God's judgment against me?'*

It is your chance now to discuss these matters. Box 11.2 offers some questions to prompt you.

Box 11.2 Suffering as cause or consequence

- Do we deserve our suffering?
- Do you believe that there is a direct causal relationship between the state of our spiritual health and the things that happen to us?
- What is the spiritual difference between suffering caused by random chance, and suffering caused by deliberate human actions?
- How can we use suffering to our own advantage?

As real as suffering is, a mature spirituality seeks to confront it honestly and courageously – not asking to be spared the suffering, but asking for the courage, wisdom, and faith to endure it and to place it in context.

The question of evil

Having looked at suffering, let's now look at evil. What is evil? Is there even such a thing as evil? There is a view of the world which sees it as the battleground between the two great conflicting forces of good and evil, literally personified as God and the Devil. We are the pawns in this great cosmic battle, and also the prize for the victor. It is logically consistent, if you believe in a personal God as the author of all that is good, to believe also in a personal devil as the author of all evil. Yet today such a view of the world does not enjoy the popularity that it once did. For the same reasons that people now are less likely to believe in a personal God who acts directly in the world, they are less likely to believe in a personalised devil who is plotting to entrap us at every turn.

However, there are people who do bad things. We are all capable of doing bad things. Some of us do very bad things, some of us do bad things often, and some of us do them occasionally. Does occasionally doing bad things make us evil? Many people have done some terrible things, but have later acknowledged their crimes, have sought and been granted forgiveness, and have redeemed themselves by going on to lead lives of commendable virtue. Indeed, it is an axiom of Christian teaching that there is no one who is beyond the hope and promise of redemption, whatever their past crimes and misdemeanours. According to the Christian tradition, we might have done evil things, but we ourselves are not evil and we are still loved by God.

Are some people inherently evil?

So, there is a distinction between doing bad things and being evil. What is that distinction? Does it even make sense to talk about being evil?

Are people evil, or is it more accurate to say that evil acts are sometimes committed by people who, through circumstance or choice, are put in a situation in which they commit acts which, in other circumstances, they would not have done?

There have been numerous psychological tests and experiments in which people have been induced to do what they ordinarily would not contemplate. What has been proven in the laboratory has, tragically, been shown also in real life. How did a country as cultured and sophisticated as Germany succumb to the horrors of Nazism? How did genocide erupt so brutally in Rwanda and Burundi? How did the US and British governments convince themselves that the torture of suspects in Guantanamo Bay and elsewhere was morally defensible? Such instances show how evil has been perpetrated by people who otherwise lay claim to moral authority. They reveal how fragile might be the veneer of our own resistance to evil. Evil can indeed seem very banal, in the arresting phrase employed by the German-American political theorist Hannah Arendt for the sub-title of her book about Adolf Eichmann, *Eichmann in Jerusalem: A Report on the Banality of Evil* (1963).

One definition of evil

Consider this definition of evil. Evil is that which knowingly and deliberately construes as good what is demonstrably not good and which is acknowledged as not good by the overwhelming majority. For example, in most people's minds the mass killing of innocent people is not a good thing. But the evil person twists the moral logic and finds justifications for asserting that it is a good thing. It is a good thing because it will cleanse society of a perceived impurity, or it is a good thing because it will enhance our economic or military supremacy. And under that delusion, the evil of genocide is justified in the minds of the perpetrators.

Most people say that torture, the deliberate and systematic inflicting of pain on another person, is evil. International standards and statutes decree that torture is evil and cannot be justified under any circumstance.

But the evil person or government turns that around and says that torture (or whatever euphemism is preferred) is a good thing because it extracts information which will protect others, or because the fear of being tortured will deter other potential offenders or terrorists. The torture is inflicted in spite of the fact that information extracted by such methods is notoriously unreliable, and in spite of the fact that its use only incites others to even greater defiance.

To conclude this examination of suffering and evil, consider human agency. We are all capable of doing bad things. We are all capable of causing pain to others, intentionally or otherwise.

Box 11.3. The human potential for evil

- What is the difference between doing bad things and being evil?
- Is the torturer doing a very bad thing, or is he essentially evil?
- Does having done a very bad thing mean that you are irredeemably evil?
- What is the place for forgiveness for perpetrators of evil?

Unit 12. A question of priorities

Although *Life Spirit* is designed so that you can do each of the individual units in separate sessions, and in whatever sequence you choose, ideally you will do this unit last of all, because it tries to encapsulate all the ideas and issues that have been addressed in the others.

Paul Tillich (1886–1965), one of the most prominent theologians in the twentieth century, believed in the importance of developing what he called a Systematic Theology. That is, a theology which was self-coherent; which tried to bring together all the different elements and ideas into an integrated whole. There are many issues and ideas to be incorporated into a fully systematic theology or personal belief system. We have looked at just some of them. What have been the questions we have touched on?

In Unit 1, we told the story of our spiritual lives, recalling the significant moments of insight and awareness; the individuals and communities who have helped to shape our personal faith; the experiences of joy and sorrow which alike have tested us; and we have pondered on what life might yet hold for us.

In Unit 2, we discussed what spirituality is, and how it is that interest in spirituality continues to flourish even while participation in organised religions is in decline. We focused on the idea that spirituality is the search for and the experience of connection. Connection with the universe; connection with others; and connection with meaning and purpose. And we developed the idea that spirituality is also about practice, ritual, and discipline. We argued that spirituality is active, not passive.

Unit 3 was about the role of personal faith. We saw how faith is not ultimately a rational phenomenon, but neither is it irrational. Faith is an attitude of the mind and the heart, it is the way we see and experience and interpret the world.

In Unit 4 we considered organised religion, acknowledging its weaknesses and limitations, but also identifying its strengths as the repository of tradition and continuity. We saw that organised religion acts as the guardian of individual spirituality, although it can also stifle creativity and personal expression.

Unit 5 was about how we make moral choices based on our religious or spiritual convictions. We considered the idea that the ability to make moral choices, to know the difference between right and wrong, is an essential element of our full humanity, as captured in the Biblical story of Adam and Eve in the Garden of Eden. And therefore freedom of will, and freedom of choice, form the bedrock of our human moral responsibility, even if that means we sometimes make bad choices.

Unit 6 concerned what is perhaps the greatest spiritual challenge of all – the fact of death. Religion and spirituality are the product of the tension between being alive and having to die; between knowing our own finitude but also knowing what it means to glimpse infinity. What happens when we die? Does death ultimately negate life, or affirm it? Is death merely a transition from one form of energy to another? These were some of the questions that we raised. What answers did you find?

In Unit 7 we considered the question of religious and spiritual authority: how do we know what to believe, and whom do we trust? Do we place our ultimate authority beyond ourselves – in a scripture or a church, in a teacher or a tradition, or are we our own final arbiter of faith?

Unit 8 looked at time and history. How did the world begin? Why did it begin? Is the universe the result of a random series of accidents, and life on Earth the most random accident of all? Or was the universe created with intentional design? We considered the misconceived conflict between science and religion in addressing those questions from different perspectives, noting that science asks *how*, but religion asks *why* – and how do I personally fit within that *why*?

Unit 9 was about beliefs. What is the importance and role of beliefs? We examined how Christianity has evolved into a tradition defined by right beliefs rather than right practice, and how beliefs can either remain an abstract theoretical construct or form the framework upon which our lives are based.

In Unit 10 we came to God: God as transcendence and God as immanence. God as personified reality, or God as poetic metaphor. We thought about the difference between believing *in* God, and holding beliefs *about* God. We asked the question, 'Is a belief in God a help or a hindrance to a mature personal spirituality?'

Then in Unit 11 we examined the reality of suffering and evil, and wondered how they can be explained away and, if not explained away, then used constructively in the creation of a realistic and honest spiritual scheme. What is the difference, we asked, between accidental suffering and deliberate evil, and what is the role of sin?

Now you have a chance to review all the units that you have been exploring. Box 12.1 asks some questions to help you in your own reflections and your group's conversation.

Box 12.1. A review of the course

- Which units did you find most challenging/helpful/enlightening/difficult, and why?
- Have your views and beliefs changed as a result of doing this course? If so, how?
- How has the sense of your own spirituality been deepened or unsettled by this course?

And what of your experience within your group?
- Were the members of your group able to be candid with each other?
- Were there surprises in what others have said?
- Were there surprises in what you yourself have said, or discovered, about your own spiritual values and beliefs?

What next?

Now we come to what is perhaps the most important question of this whole course. It is a question expressed in just two words. *So what?*

You have done this course. So what? What will it mean now for who you are, for how you understand yourself and your place in the universe? What will it mean for how you live, and how you put into practice the things that you have learned? How will this make a lasting difference in your spiritual life?

There are lots of courses you can do, on many different topics and for many different reasons. You do them, you enjoy doing them, perhaps you even get a certificate at the end to prove that you have done them. You don't get a certificate to prove you have done this course. Doing this course will not qualify you to get a job, and you are unlikely to get a pay rise because of it! Yet it is possible that this course might have changed your life. It might have opened up a door to your understanding which hitherto had remained firmly shut.

The real question is not, 'What door has this course opened up?' The real question is, 'What doors am I going to open now?' The real question is not about what has already been. It is about the future. It is about the 'So What?'

You could conclude that you have enjoyed this course, that you have got something out of it, but now you will forget about it. If that is what happens, doing this course won't have been a waste of time: it can have been interesting and valuable and all of that, but it won't necessarily lead to anything else. It won't necessarily help you in your continuing spiritual quest. There won't be a 'So What?'

Perhaps, though, for you there will be a 'So What'. You can use this course to re-shape the day-to-day realities of your spiritual life. Having talked about the ideas behind your spirituality, you can now put those ideas into practice. You will have realised that spirituality is about doing, not just thinking and talking. And not doing just once, but doing over and over, again and again, the ritual of doing, as we explored in Unit 2.

What will you do? It might be that you will pursue further study. It might be that you will resolve to meditate regularly, or commit yourself to attending a place of worship with intention and regularity. You might choose a physical discipline like yoga, or a martial art or walking meditation. You might have come to the realisation that what you need to do is look beyond yourself and become involved in work for the benefit of the wider world, and that you must do that not only for the practical benefit that such involvement will bring to others, but for the spiritual benefit that it will bring to you.

There is no shortage of options for action. There is no absolute right or wrong. There is only what is right or wrong for you. Box 12.2 offers some guidelines to help you to choose.

Box 12.2. Next steps

- Choose something possible and sustainable and which you can fit into your present life. You might think you should become a hermit living in a cave. But how realistic is that, given that you are married with three children, have a responsible job and a mortgage?
- Choose something which will make some demands on you. No, that does not contradict the first guideline. If you want to be serious about your spirituality, you will need to accept that it will be likely to change your life.
- Choose something which you can introduce yourself to at whatever level is appropriate for who and where you are now, but which you can commit yourself to at deeper levels as you become more accomplished.
- Do you want to commit yourself to your spiritual practice for a specified period of time, so that you can review your progress?
- How will you hold yourself accountable to your practice, so that you do not fall away in your observance of it?

Take some time now to write down what you want to do. Then, when you are ready, share your ideas with each other as you feel able.

......

You have written down and shared with your group what you think will work for you, and how you intend to continue holding yourself accountable. Remember to be gentle with yourself. If you forget to observe your practice one day or one week, don't give up. You have not failed. You can simply return to your chosen spiritual practice with renewed determination.

Perhaps your group will decide to continue meeting at regular or occasional intervals so that you can check in with each other, support each other, continue to learn from each other.

Final exercises

Which of the four sayings in each of the following categories do you most agree with?

Discuss your answers in your group.

Religion
1. Religion is the opiate of the people.
2. Religion is the force that holds humanity together.
3. Religion has done more harm in the world than anything else.
4. There is only one religion, although there are a hundred versions of it.

Belief
1. We are what we believe.
2. They who know nothing will believe anything.
3. What you believe is the thing you do, not the thing you think.
4. For those who believe, no proof is necessary. For those who don't believe, no proof is possible.

God
1. God is a verb, not a noun.
2. Absence of proof is not proof of absence.
3. God created the universe.
4. God is a dangerous delusion.

Spirituality
1. Spirituality is the desire to be holy rather than happy.
2. Spirituality is connection.
3. We are not human beings with a spiritual life, we are spiritual beings with a human life.
4. Spirituality is for people who don't want to study physics.

Appendix A. Suggestions for the group leader

The role of the leader in a *Life Spirit* group is to introduce and facilitate each session so that each person derives the maximum benefit from identifying, articulating, and developing their own experiences and beliefs. The leader should not dominate the discussion or try to impose his or her views. Rather the leader should seek to guide the discussion, to ensure that all members participate as they feel able, and to manage the practicalities of the group.

It might be useful to have two leaders. If this is the case, you should agree beforehand who will take primary leadership for each part of the session, recognising that the role of the other will be to support, possibly intervene, observe, and attend to practical details. After each session, it would be valuable to spend some time in debriefing: what worked and what did not, how you felt at various times, what could be improved.

The ideal size of the group, including leaders, is no fewer than six and no more than 12. It might be that all members of the group are already well known to each other, or that some are well known and others not, or that all are previously strangers to each other. If there are pre-existing friendships within the group, it is important to ensure that they do not interfere with the cohesion of the whole group. It might be desirable to manage the seating arrangement so that people sit next to different people each time.

It is important to provide comfortable seating, adequate warmth, and good lighting. Part of the occasion might be the sharing of a simple meal (either at the beginning or the end), so you will need appropriate facilities. The meal should not dominate the time spent together, but should be a way of encouraging informal sharing and bringing members of the group into a stronger sense of mutual trust and enjoyment.

At the start of the course, it is important to establish a covenant of expected behaviour and mutual responsibilities, to which all members of the group subscribe. Each group's covenant is open to negotiation by its members, but here are some suggested guidelines:

- **Treat each other with respect**. Members should share their own ideas without attempting to force them on the group, and should listen attentively as others share their thoughts.

- **Attendance**. It is hoped that people will attend all sessions, or inform the leader in advance if unable to attend a particular session.

- **Punctuality**. Sessions should start and end at agreed times. Two hours is probably about the right length.

- **Confidentiality**. Members should feel able to share their experiences, views, and feelings knowing that confidentiality will be observed by their fellows.

- **The right to pass**. People should be encouraged to speak for as long as is comfortable for them. However, each person is entitled *not* to speak, if that is their wish. Some leaders like to provide a token, such as a smooth pebble or a pine cone, which gives the person holding it the right to speak.

You might have drinks (wine and a non-alcoholic alternative) and snacks available as people arrive. Allow no more than five minutes for latecomers before starting the session. You might start with the light meal, or leave that until the end. You could say a grace at the start of the meal, or invite other members of the group to do so. Some suggested words are provided in Appendix B.

There should be a feeling of sharing a special, safe, even sacred, space. Sessions might begin with the lighting of a candle, or by each participant lighting a tea-light.

Opening words and rituals are suggested in Appendix B, together with a selection of readings for you to use according to your preference. But as the leader you are free to devise your own opening rituals as you see fit. You may take responsibility for this at the start of each session, or responsibility may be shared by the members of the group. Some groups might like to have the same opening ritual each time, and others might like to vary it.

You might then invite each person to take no more than one minute each to share how they are feeling, naming a cause for joy, sadness, weariness, or worry that they are bringing to the group and which they want the group to be aware of. Be sure that each of these contributions is brief. Find a way to deal with this gently, so that no-one speaks for too long.

At the end of the session you might invite each person to share how they now feel, or to share with others what has been important to them during the session. Try to ensure that people speak only briefly.

There are some suggestions for closing words in Appendix B. You may choose to do the same ritual at the end of each session for the sake of continuity, or use something different for the sake of variety.

Appendix B. Rituals and readings

Candle lighting

....

We light this candle as a symbol of faith.
By its light may our vision be illumined.
By its warmth may our fellowship be encouraged.
And by its flame may our yearnings for peace, justice,
and the life of the spirit be enkindled.
David Usher

....

As we gather, we light this candle as a symbol of hope.
May the inner light within each of us be kindled each day.
May the light of truth and goodness be a part of our lives constantly.
May we seek always to bring light wherever the deep shadows fall.

We light this candle as a symbol of the spark of life
which abides within us and around us.
May it be as a light in a dark night,
a light in a window that welcomes the weary traveller home.
May it be as a light in the hand of a trusted friend, that guides us along
    the path.
May it be as the light in the face of one we love, bright with joy.

Linda Hart

....

May the light that we now kindle
inspire us to use our powers
to heal and not to harm,
to help and not to hinder,
to bless and not to curse,
to uphold the Spirit of Freedom.
Peter Teets

We light this candle, symbol of the Light within us and around us.
May this gathering enlighten our hearts and our minds and our souls.
And may the Inner Light of the Spirit be kindled by our time together.
Stephen Lingwood

Let this light remind us of the sacred flame of life that blazes within.
Constant, yet ever-changing. Burning, yet never consumed.
O inner light of soul and spirit, lead our minds to greater understanding,
lead our hearts to love more fully,
and lead our hands to create justice.
Andy Pakula

As I light this candle upon which we can focus in our own, individual ways,
may we remember that it is something we share.
May it remind us of that Greater Light which we seek within ourselves and
in our world.
As we share the journey – alone and together – let us not lose sight of this
Greater Light.
June Pettitt

We light our candle in the name of peace.
May its flame be a reminder of the warmth of community.
May its light be a guide to bring love to our hearts.
We light our chalice in the name of peace.
Daniel Costley

Opening words

....

We have crept out of our close and crowded houses into the night and
morning, and we see what majestic beauties daily wrap us in their
bosom. . . . These enchantments are medicinal, they sober and heal us.
These are plain pleasures, kindly and native to us. We come to our own,
and make friends with matter. . . . We never can part with it; the mind
loves its old home: as water to our thirst, so is the rock, the ground, to
our eyes, and hands, and feet.
Ralph Waldo Emerson, from "Nature", Essays: Second Series (1844)

....

Come into this circle of community. Come into this sacred space.
Be not tentative.
Bring your whole self!
Bring the joy that makes your heart sing.
Bring your kindness and your compassion.
Bring also your sorrow, your pain.
Bring your brokenness and your disappointments.
Spirit of love and mystery: help us to recognise the spark of the divine
    that resides within each of us.
May we know the joy of wholeness.
May we know the joy of being together.
Andy Pakula

....

We enter into this time and this place to join our hearts and minds
    together.
We come to this place: the doors open, the heat comes on, biscuits are
    laid, the water heats, and you all come.
What is it that we come here seeking? Many things, too many to
    mention them all.
Yet, it is likely that some common longings draw us to be with one
    another.
To remember what is most important in life.

To be challenged to live more truly, more deeply, to live with integrity
and kindness and with hope and love.
To feel the company of those who seek a common path.
To be renewed in our faith in the promise of this life.
To be strengthened and to find the courage to continue to do what we
must do, day after day, world without end.
Linda Hart

We come to offer thanksgiving for that greatest of miracles,
the miracle that Life is.
As we breathe in the peace of this time and place,
and as we release some of the stress of everyday living,
let us allow ourselves to wonder.
Out of the experience of wonder comes religion.
Out of religion comes the strength we need to take us forward
in a perplexing world.
June Pettitt

Even if your longings are different from these, you are welcome here.
Even if you do not have the strength and the courage to pass along, you
are welcome here. You are welcome in your grief and your joy to be within
this circle of companions. We gather here. It is good to be together.
Linda Hart

Here we gather.
We gather for all the same reasons that we gather week after week.

To lift up the gift of life that is ours.
To remember that life is holy.
To pray for healing and hope in the midst of trouble.
To give thanks for the blessings that surround us.

Today especially we lift these up: the gift of life, the holiness that
surrounds us, the troubles and blessings.

As we remember and honour those who have given themselves to the cause of war in its intensity and terror, we remember those who have given their lives in hope of a new day of peace.

In the quiet of our gathering, may we lift up our hearts in grateful thanksgiving for their lives, and for the promise of peace that they mean.

Peter Teets

We come together, seeking a reality beyond our narrow selves; that
    binds us in compassion, love, and understanding to other human
    beings, and to the interdependent web of all living things.
May our hearts and minds be opened to the power and the insight that
    weaves together the scattered threads of our experience, and help us
    remember the Wholeness of which we are part.
We come together to renew our faith in the holiness, the goodness, the
    beauty of life.
To reaffirm the way of the open mind and the full heart; to rekindle the
    flame of memory and hope; and to reclaim the vision of an earth
    more fair, with all her people one.
David Usher

Bring your hopes and anticipations.
Bring your joys and celebrations.
Bring your sorrows and lamentations.
Bring your faith and adorations.
Bring to this hour of worship all that makes your life real and meaningful,
that you may be blessed by communion with the lives of others.
David Usher

Because we are finite, we lift up our eyes to the infinite sky, and feel
  wonder and awe.
Because we have stumbled, we take the tender hand which beckons us
  to rise, and feel strength and reassurance.
Because we are lonely, we reach out to those around us, and feel
  warmth and acceptance.
Because we are human, we do all of these things, and in our worship
  feel the presence of the divine.
David Usher

Open your hearts to the wonder of worship.
Open your minds to the eternal quest for meaning and truth.
Open your eyes to the miracle of creation.
Open your arms to the embrace of your fellow men and women.
Open your souls, and let the divine sweep in.
David Usher

We come together from many directions, following a myriad of routes
  and roads of life to get to this point.
From here we will go our different ways in different directions.
May our time together for this hour strengthen us and our resolve to
  travel the right road on the trail of Truth.
As we speed on, let us not forget our fellow travellers: to stop and help
  if they're fallen; to guide them wisely if they're lost; to encourage
  them in their own journey.
May our onward journey be as challenging and exciting as that so far.
Martin Gienke

Readings

I am a believer in God, in 'X', in something beyond definition.

Churches and sects, religions of all kinds are monopolies. God is like the water that flows down the mountainside and fills the brooks and rivers.

There come certain men who bottle the waters, some in ugly bottles, some in beautiful ones, and these bottles they sell, saying that 'only this water will quench your thirst'.

That it does quench thirst we will not deny, but the water is often stale and flat and the sparkle has gone out of it.

You can drink better from the hollow of your hands kneeling by the brook.

In China we bottle it with mystic writings and flavour it with cinnamon and spices.

Here, in England, it is bottled without much regard to the water, but with great care as to the shape of the bottle.

I go always to the brook.

Edgar Wallace (The Clue of the New Pin)

We see barriers erected between people of different lands, We see sheets of steel and towers of concrete called Protection. We see boundaries policed, we watch men, women, and children running from hunger and persecution, looking for a gap in the wall ...

Something there is that doesn't love a wall ... We see walls of fear – fear of the young, fear of the stranger, fear of sexuality that is different, fear of the educated, fear of the poor, fear of the Muslim, fear of the Jew – fear upon fear, endless and perpetuating, and we offer our silent prayer that solid walls of fear will crumble to dust.

Something there is that doesn't love a wall ... We hear the language of separation, the jingoistic chant, the racial slur, words of indifference and dismissal, words arranged for the purpose of exclusion, words that sting and taunt, words that lie. Let us find words that ring with love and truthfulness, that reach out through the emptiness of separation.

Something there is that doesn't love a wall ... We see the deluded barriers of the mind protecting self, we see relationships stripped of affection as one person becomes closed to another. We see people trapped in misunderstanding, old hurts re-ignited, bricks placed higher on the wall, goodwill and trust suspended. And we ask for boundaries that are not impenetrable, through which light can shine and distance be dissolved.

Something there is that doesn't love a wall .... And when we need these boundaries for our own well-being, let us know them for what they are, use them wisely and kindly, recognising our own vulnerability and that of others – so each of us can find the space for retreat and succour, find that peace that passes all understanding, and be renewed with strength and love for the task of living life joyfully in communion with all others.

Margaret Kirk

What is blasphemy?
To live on the unpaid labour of others – that is blasphemy.
To enslave your fellow man, to put chains on his body – that is blasphemy.
To enslave the minds of men, to put manacles upon the brain, padlocks upon the lips – that is blasphemy.
To deny what you believe to be true, to admit to be true what you believe to be a lie – that is blasphemy.
To strike the weak and the unprotected, in order that you may gain the applause of the ignorant and superstitious mob – that is blasphemy.
To persecute the intelligent few, at the command of the ignorant many – that is blasphemy.
To forge chains, to build dungeons, for honest fellow-men – that is blasphemy.
To pollute the souls of children with the dogma of eternal pain – that is blasphemy.
To violate your conscience – that is blasphemy.
Robert Ingersoll

This is the true joy in life, the being used for a purpose recognised by yourself as a mighty one, the being a force of nature instead of a feverish, selfish, little clod of ailments and grievances complaining that the world will not devote itself to making you happy.

I am of the opinion that my life belongs to the whole community, and as long as I live it is my privilege to do for it whatever I can.

I want to be thoroughly used up when I die, for the harder I work the more I live. I rejoice in life for its own sake.

Life is no brief candle to me. It is a sort of splendid torch which I've got hold of for the moment, and I want to make it burn as brightly as possible before handing it on to future generations.

George Bernard Shaw

....

In a cemetery, once, I found a soothing epitaph. The name of the deceased had been scoured away by wind and rain, but there was a carving of a tree with roots and branches (a classic nineteenth-century motif) and among them the words *'She attended well and faithfully to a few worthy things'*. At first this seemed a little meagre, a little stingy on the part of her survivors, but I wrote it down and have thought about it since, and now I can't imagine a more proud or satisfying legacy. *'She attended well and faithfully to a few worthy things.'*

Every day I stand in danger of being struck by lightning and having the obituary in the local paper say for all the world to see: *'She attended frantically and ineffectually to a great many unimportant, meaningless details.'*

How do you want your obituary to read?

'He got all the dishes washed and dried before playing with his children in the evening.'

'She balanced her chequebook with meticulous precision and never missed a day of work – missed a lot of sunsets, missed a lot of love, missed a lot of risk, missed a lot – but her money was in order.'

'She answered all her calls, all her email, all her voice-mail, but along the way she forgot to answer the call to service and compassion, and forgiveness, first and foremost of herself.'

'He gave and forgave sparingly, without radical intention, without passion or conviction.'

'She could not, or would not, hear the calling of her heart.'

How will it read, how does it read, and if you had to name a few worthy things to which you attend well and faithfully, what, I wonder, would they be?

Victoria Safford

....

People seek retreats for themselves, houses in the country, sea-shores and mountains; and you too are wont to desire such things very much. But this is altogether a mark of the most common sort of person, for it is in your power, whenever you shall choose, to retire into yourself. For nowhere, either with more quiet or more freedom from trouble, do you retire than into your own soul, particularly when you have within you such thoughts that by looking into them you are immediately in perfect tranquillity. And I affirm that tranquillity is nothing else than the good ordering of the mind. Constantly, then, give to yourself this retreat, and renew yourself. Let your principles be brief and fundamental, which, as soon as you shall recur to them, will be sufficient to cleanse the soul completely, and to send you back from all discontent with the things to which you return.

This then remains. Remember to retire into this little territory of your own, and above all, do not distract or strain yourself, but be free, and look at things as a person, as a human being, as a citizen, as a mortal.

Marcus Aurelius (Meditations, 161–180 CE))

I feel the earth beneath my feet, and I know that I am part of the earth;
and it is good.

I feel my heart beating, and I know that I am sustained by all that is
   around me;
and it is good.

I feel my breath, and I know that I am alive;
and it is good.

I reach out and touch all those who are around me, and I know that I
   am not alone;
and it is good.

And for all these things, I offer my thanks to the universe;
and it is good.

Jill McAllister

I am a part of the earth.
I am a part of the solid, unshakeable, immutable rock of the mountain;
a part of the stark, rain-washed slabs of slate,
a part of the walls of wet and weathered grit-stone,
a part of the crumbling granite of shining boulders.
I am part of what makes the green rounded hill with its splashes of
   laughing yellow gorse.

Through the earth I am aware of what I am:
all that is firmly fixed and endures forever,
all that is shifting imperceptibly,
being gently folded and unfolded,
all that holds the possibility of shattering violence and eruption;
all that is contained in Is, and Was, and Shall Be.

For such awareness, coming from the earth,
I give my thanks today for the earth, and my part in it.

Elizabeth Birtles

For I have learned to look on Nature,
not as in the hour of thoughtless youth;
but hearing oftentimes the still, sad music of humanity,
not harsh nor grating, though of ample power to chasten and subdue.
And I have felt a presence that disturbs me
with the joy of elevated thoughts;
A sense sublime of something far more deeply inter-fused,
whose dwelling is the light of setting suns,
and the round ocean and the living air,
and the blue sky and in the mind of man:
A motion and a spirit that impels all thinking things,
all objects of all thought, and rolls through all things.
Therefore am I still a lover of the meadows and the woods, and
    mountains;
And of all that we behold from this green earth;
Of all the mighty world of eye and ear,
both of what they half create, and what perceive;
Well pleased to recognise in nature and the language of the sense,
the anchor of my purest thoughts, the nurse, the guide, the guardian of
    my heart,
and soul of all my moral being.
William Wordsworth (Tintern Abbey, 1798)

Graces

. . . .

In a sometimes hungry and sometimes lonely world, for this food and
this fellowship we offer our reverent thanks.

. . . .

We gather this evening to share this food together, and to share our
spiritual journeys. May we do so with reverence and gratitude in our
hearts. May we be touched by the spirit of holiness which blesses our
togetherness.

For the goodness of the earth and the labours of others which have brought us this food we are about to share, we offer our reverent thanks. As we receive, so may we give as we pass the bounties of our labours on to others.

Closing words

May the love of God surround us,
may the peace of God assure us,
and may the blessing of God rest with us until we gather here again.
Ant Howe

There is a place of peace, a place of wisdom, a place of love.
May this sacred centre be your guide.
May it be your strength for the journey.
May it fill you with hope when all seems hopeless.
And may it lead you to know the sacredness in all.
Andy Pakula

Walk bravely
facing the truth
with goodness in your heart
and beauty in your actions.
Martin Gienke

Eternal Spirit, we are thankful for this time together.
As we depart and take our service to the world,
may our hearts and minds be supported
by the loving community we have shared today.
Let there be peace among us, now and forever.
Daniel Costley

Be aware of your breathing.
Pay attention to how you are feeling right now.
Be aware of your stillness.
How often do you allow yourself such times?
Be aware of your physical self, and also of your thoughts, your feelings.
Ask yourself, What does it mean to you to be a spiritual being?
How do you or will you make that real in your life?
What difference does it make in your life?
And may the serenity of this moment remain with you.
So may it be.
David Usher

Appendix C. Guide to the units: questions and exercises

Unit 1. Your Odyssey

1.1. Your religious background
- What kind of religious upbringing, if any, did you have?
- Have you stayed within the faith of your childhood? Or have you ventured elsewhere? Or have you abandoned organised religion altogether?
- If you did not have a religious upbringing, what has drawn you to consider spiritual questions now?
- Have there been times of particular crisis, celebration, joy or pain in your life which have challenged your assumptions about what you do or don't believe?

1.2. Choices you have made
- What was the path that led to your career or your present situation?
- How did you choose where you live?
- How have you chosen to start or end the significant relationships in your life?
- Do you feel that you have been in control of the choices in your life, or does it feel as though choices have been made for you?
- Have you made choices that you now regret?

1.3. How do you respond to life's challenges?
- Think of a sad or challenging event in your life so far. Did you deal with it well? If you are willing, briefly share details with your group.
- Did you grow through that experience, or have you been unable to put down the burden of your grief or frustration?
- What role did your personal faith play in helping you through the experience, and how did the experience affect your faith?

1.4. Facing your future
- How long do you expect to live?
- What do you fear about growing older?
- Are there things that you specifically want to accomplish in your life?
- What measures will you use to evaluate how well you have lived?

1.5. The life and times of the spirit
  - When or why or how has your spirituality been important to you?
  - Can you recognise times when you have been spiritually active and other times when you have been preoccupied with other calls on your energies?
  - Think about the times when you have been spiritually active, and the times when you have been spiritually inactive. Can you discern a qualitative difference in how you have felt about your life at those times?

Unit 2. What is spirituality?

2.1. From public religion to private spirituality
  - Is the contemporary weakening of traditional religion a good thing?
  - What influences do you think have contributed to this shift from the authority of a central Church to individuals being free to choose from a supermarket of spiritualities?
  - Who are the spiritual authorities today?
  - What has been gained and what has been lost in the breakdown of spiritual practice?
  - Has this shift made us more open to other spiritualities?

2.2. Connecting with the universe
  - Have you had any 'WOW' moments that you are willing to share with your group, when you have felt connected with the universe?
  - How do you respond to the beauty of creation?
  - What is your spiritual response to the vastness and the timelessness of the universe?

2.3. Connecting with meaning
  - Does life have meaning?
  - What gives meaning to your life?
  - Is there tension between your answers to the first and second questions?
  - Is it possible to have a meaningful life in isolation from other people?

2.4. Connecting with practice
  - Do you agree that spirituality requires practice?
  - What practices do you already do?
  - What have you tried which did not work for you?
  - What might you like to try?
  - What benefit would you hope to derive from such new practices?

Unit 3. The role of personal faith

3.1. An article of faith
- Can you provide a single statement of your own belief?
- Why do you hold that belief?
- Why it is important to you?

3.2. Ways of seeing the world
- Is the world rich or poor?
- Can you identify reasons why you see the world as either a place of emptiness or a place of fullness?
- Are some ways of seeing the world better than others?
- What things give you ultimate hope?

3.3. A person of faith
- What do you admire about this person?
- How are that person's actions consistent with his or her personal faith?
- Do you discern inconsistencies in that person, and do those inconsistencies add to or detract from their overall impact as a person of faith?
- Would you like to be more like him or her, and, if so, how would you need to change?

Unit 4. The role of organised religion

4.1. Organised religion: good or bad?
- Have you had a good or a bad experience of organised religion?
- Are you basically in favour of religion, or do you think it is pernicious?
- If you are neither wholly for nor wholly against religion, what do you see as its good points and its bad points?

4.2. The need to belong
- What are the benefits and disadvantages of being a committed sports fan?
- What are the benefits and disadvantages of being a committed church-goer?
- What similarities and differences are there between attending church and following a sport such as football?

4.3. The role of ritual

Think of a group to which you belong, or an activity that you regularly do, and identify rituals and modes of behaviour of that group or that activity.
- Does it involve a dress code?
- Do you have certain ways to address each other?
- How did you learn the rituals?
- How do you teach them to newcomers?

Recall a situation in which you were a visitor and there were rituals and practices which everyone else seemed to know and understand, but you had no idea what was going on. It might have attendance at a place of worship, or it might have been a concert or a social situation.
- Can you identify what those practices were?
- Did they seem strange?
- How did you – if at all – learn those practices?

4.4. In the final analysis ...
- Do you think the world would be a better place if there were no organised religion? Or is the existence of organised religion an inevitable manifestation of the essential human need to explore and give collective expression to the fact of our spirituality?
- Could you be spiritual all by yourself?
- How has your understanding of religion changed as a result of this unit?

Unit 5. Making moral choices

5.1. Adam and Eve: the archetypal story of Free Will
- Was Adam and Eve's sin disobedience, or was it the inevitable need to fulfil their humanity?
- Would you want to live in a state of morality-free innocence if it meant surrendering the ability to make your own choices?
- Is the knowledge of Good and Evil the defining point of adult humanity?
- Do you know other stories and myths which have the same theme as the story of Adam and Eve?

5.2. What is the basis of your own morality?

- Do you believe that there are moral absolutes, to be invoked and applied in all circumstances?
- Are you a moral relativist, trying to weigh up the costs and benefits in each situation?
- Are you a utilitarian, believing in whatever promotes the greatest good for the greatest number?
- What is your moral compass?

5.3. Motivation and conscience

- Describe a time when you have done something and your motives have been misconstrued – by yourself or by others.
- Is morality primarily determined by the action itself, or by the motivation for the action?
- Consider the concept of 'conscience'. What is it? How is it informed by the larger communities of which you are part: by religion, by your particular social set, or by society in general?
- Do you behave morally for the intrinsic value of doing so, or because you fear the consequences of not doing so?

Unit 6. Facing death

6.1. Personal perspectives on death

- Is this life a once-only preparation for eternal life?
- Is this life one episode in a series of lives which will lead to eventual release from this world?
- Is this life all there is, and is death the end of all personal consciousness?
- What are your reasons for believing as you do? Or are your beliefs based on wishful thinking?
- Do you have any direct experience which has led you to your beliefs?

6.2. Negation or fulfilment?

- Is death the negation of life, making it meaningless? Or is death the fulfilment of life, making it meaningful?
- For you personally, does the prospect of death cast a shadow over life or shine a light on it?
- To what extent is it the purpose of religion and faith to enable the individual to be reconciled with death?

6.3. The experience of bereavement, and its impact on faith
- What were the sources of your comfort and strength in that time of sadness?
- Was there a discrepancy between what you believed and what you experienced?
- Did the experience affect your faith, or vice versa?

Unit 7. By whose authority?

7.1. Whom do you trust?
Think about the people whom you regard as authorities, in whatever sphere: politics, medicine, or religion, for example.
- Can you identify characteristics which they have in common?
- What is likely to make you believe someone?
- Which is more important to you – what is being said, or who is saying it?
- Which people do you instinctively trust, and which do you instinctively distrust?

7.2. The authority of the Bible and other scriptures
- Do you believe that the Bible is the literal word of God, or is it a book with uniquely great religious value?
- Is it one great book among many books of scripture, or is it irrelevant to your personal spirituality?
- Are there other books, or particular writers, which have made a significant impact on your spiritual life and have become part of your personal scriptures?

7.3. Are you a pilgrim or a pioneer?
- How do you instinctively respond to a person who claims spiritual authority?
- Some people do seem to have an air of spiritual authority. What are the characteristics of such a person?
- What makes one person a pilgrim and another a pioneer?
- What are the advantages and disadvantages of being a pilgrim?
- What are the advantages and disadvantages of being a pioneer?
- Can you be both a pilgrim and a pioneer?
- Are there more pilgrims or more pioneers in your group?

7.4. Sources of authority
- How much do you trust your own spiritual authority, and why?
- What is the role of spiritual community in helping you to decide what is true?
- How do you know if something is true?
- What authority, if any, do you ascribe to this course?

Unit 8. Time and history

8.1. What does the creation myth mean to you?
- What do you believe is the relationship between God and the creation of the world?
- What can be learned from creation stories such as those found in the Book of Genesis?
- Are you familiar with other religious myths about how the world began?
- Are science and religion complementary or adversarial?
- Which are more important to you – the 'how' questions of science or the 'why' questions of religion?

8.2. The end of the world
- What do you think is the future of Earth?
- How does that ultimate future affect how you live now?
- Does it make you fatalistic or hopeful?
- Is your personal spiritual salvation separate from the future of the planet, or intensely dependent upon it?

8.3. Ourselves in the context of eternity
- To what extent is your personal story determined by the story of the world?
- If your personal safety could be guaranteed, what epoch in the history of the world would you like to visit, and why?
- Describe your vision of heaven on earth.

Unit 9. The importance of belief

9.1. Believing *that* ...
Do you answer Yes or No to the following assertions?
- God created the world.
- Jesus was crucified by the Roman authorities.
- My death will be the end of all of my personal consciousness.
- The Bible is the infallible Word of God.
- God will bring the world to an apocalyptic end and establish his kingdom of the righteous for all time.

9.2. Believing *in*

- What do you believe in? Can you identify just one thing that you believe in which governs your life and to which you commit yourself?
- What does that belief mean in terms of how you live?
- What are the beliefs *that* which follow from your belief *in*?
- How important is it that what you believe in is based on what is objectively true?

9.3. The bricks of belief in the home of faith

- Is being a person of faith about holding the right beliefs?
- Is being a person of faith about believing in something to which you commit yourself?
- Are beliefs intellectual propositions, or emotional attachments?
- Write down and share with your group five statements beginning with the words 'I believe *that*...'. And one statement which begins with the words 'I believe *in*...'. How is your belief *in* statement related to your belief *that* statements?

Unit 10. God

10.1. A brief history of God

- What roles has God been given? For example, king, shepherd, judge? Can you cite further examples?
- What human emotions have been attributed to God?
- How does God interfere with or control human destiny?
- How did God create the world?

10.2. Metaphors for God

Do any of the following metaphors resonate with your own experience?
- God as Judge
- God as Father
- God as Mother
- God as King
- God as Warrior
- God as Shepherd
- God as Law Giver
- God as Shepherd
- God as Teacher

Can you think of any other metaphors for God?

10.3. Does God exist?

- Can you have a relationship with something that does not exist?
- What kind of relationship might that be, and how do you cultivate it?
- Does God respond?
- How do you know God?

10.4. God in daily life

- Think about the beliefs that you have previously shared *about* God, and consider their impact on your daily practice of spirituality.
- In other words, how do you translate your beliefs *about* God into believing *in* God?

Unit 11. Suffering and evil

11.1. Suffering as a condition of life

- How do you explain suffering?
- Do you think God is not all-good, is not all-powerful – or do you think that suffering is not real?
- Can you think of instances in which you have experienced suffering in the realm of human relationships, either as its cause or its victim?
- How has your own suffering affected you spiritually, for better or for worse?

11.2. Suffering as cause or consequence

- Do we deserve our suffering?
- Do you believe that there is a direct causal relationship between the state of our spiritual health and the things which happen to us?
- What is the spiritual difference between suffering caused by random chance, and suffering caused by deliberate human actions?
- How can we use suffering to our own advantage?

11.3. The human potential for evil

- What is the difference between doing bad things and being evil?
- Is the torturer doing a very bad thing, or is he essentially evil?
- Does having done a very bad thing mean that you are irredeemably evil?
- What is the place for forgiveness for perpetrators of evil?

Unit 12. A question of priorities

12.1. A review of the course
- Which units did you find most challenging/helpful/enlightening/difficult, and why?
- How have your views and beliefs changed as a result of doing this course?
- How has the sense of your own spirituality been deepened or unsettled by this course?

And what of your experience within your group?
- Were the members of your group able to be candid with each other?
- Were there surprises in what others have said?
- Were there surprises in what you yourself have said, or discovered, about your own spiritual values and beliefs?

12.2. Next steps
- Choose something possible and sustainable and which you can fit into your present life. You might think you should become a hermit living in a cave. But how realistic is that, given that you are married with three children, have a responsible job and a mortgage?
- Choose something which will make some demands on you. No, that does not contradict the first guideline. If you want to be serious about your spirituality, you will need to accept that it will be likely to change your life.
- Choose something which you can introduce yourself to at whatever level is appropriate for who and where you are now, but which you can commit yourself to at deeper levels as you become more accomplished.
- Do you want to commit yourself to your spiritual practice for a specified period of time, so that you can review your progress?
- How will you hold yourself accountable to your practice, so that you do not fall away in your observance of it?

Final exercises

Which of the four sayings in each of the categories do you most agree with?

Discuss your answers in your group.

Religion
1. Religion is the opiate of the people.
2. Religion is the force that holds humanity together.
3. Religion has done more harm in the world than anything else.
4. There is only one religion, though there are a hundred versions of it.

Belief
1. We are what we believe.
2. They who know nothing will believe anything.
3. What you believe is the thing you do, not the thing you think.
4. For those who believe, no proof if necessary. For those who don't believe, no proof is possible.

God
1. God is a verb, not a noun.
2. Absence of proof is not proof of absence.
3. God created the universe.
4. God is a dangerous delusion.

Spirituality
1. Spirituality is the desire to be holy rather than happy.
2. Spirituality is connection.
3. We are not human beings with a spiritual life, we are spiritual beings with a human life.
4. Spirituality is for people who don't want to study physics.

Blank pages for personal notes

Blank pages for personal notes

Blank pages for personal notes

Blank pages for personal notes

Blank pages for personal notes

Blank pages for personal notes

24/5/16

Lightning Source UK Ltd.
Milton Keynes UK
UKOW02f1020160516

274327UK00001B/131/P